THE WAYFARER

RE-IMAGINING THE POSSIBLE ✦ CHARTING THE WAY FOR CHANGE

> *"We cannot live only for ourselves.*
> *A thousand fibers connect us with our fellow men."*
> – HERMAN MELVILLE

Since 2012, *The Wayfarer* has been offering literature, interviews, and art with the intention to inspire our readers, enrich their lives, and highlight the power for agency and change-making that each individual holds.

By our definition, a wayfarer is one whose inner compass is ever-oriented to truth, wisdom, healing, and beauty in their own wandering.

The Wayfarer's mission as a publication is to foster a community of contemplative voices and provide readers with resources and perspectives that support them in their own journey.

As we move into our 10th year, in the face of these frightening times we must endure, we renew our commitment to our readers to be a space of solace and our pledge to advocate for marginalized communities, the arts, and environmental conservation.

A LAND ACKNOWLEDGMENT

The offices of *The Wayfarer Magazine* and Homebound Publications—the publishing company under which it falls—are situated in the small fishing village of Stonington, Connecticut on lands once occupied by the Pequot and the Mohegan people (known in present-day as the Mashantucket Pequot Tribal Nation and the Mohegan Nation respectively) whose lands were taken from them by force and duplicity. We honor this history and hold it within our minds and hearts as we midwife our creative endeavors from this space on the Connecticut shoreline.

The names of the land as quoted within this essay collection have gone by many names in the languages of both the native peoples for whom they were home and eventually the European settlers. But let us also remember that the land exists as a sentient being beyond labels, borders, and quantification.

WWW.THEWAYFARER.HOMEBOUNDPUBLICATIONS.COM

THE WAYFARER

RE-IMAGINING THE POSSIBLE ✷ CHARTING THE WAY FOR CHANGE

FOUNDER AND EDITOR-IN-CHIEF
L.M. Browning

MANAGING EDITOR & THE MINDFUL KITCHEN
Heidi Barr

EDITORS
Theodore Richards

POETRY EDITOR
Amy Nawrocki

ASSOCIATE EDITOR
Eric D. Lehman

STAFF WRITERS
David K. Leff
Iris Graville
Jason Kirkey

READER
Marianne Browning
J.K. McDowell

CONTACT US

The Wayfarer Magazine
13 Old South Street, Suite 2G Northampton, MA 01060
thewayfarer@homeboundpublications.com

SUBSCRIBE

www.thewayfarer.homeboundpublications.com
or orders@homeboundpublications.com

1 **LETTER FROM** *The Editor*
BY L.M. BROWNING

3 **SECTION ONE:**
THE WAYFARERS

33 **SECTION TWO**
COLUMNS

47 **SECTION THREE:**
ESSAYS

64 **SECTION FOUR:**
MINDFUL KITCHEN

69 **SECTION FIVE:**
POETRY

LETTER FROM THE EDITOR

In 2012, we released our first issue of *The Wayfarer Magazine* into the world. In 2022, we mark the 10th anniversary of the publication. Since then, the vision has evolved, the staff has grown, but the ideals revolving at the center of the publication have remained and matured. For me personally, what this circle of creatives means has also progressed. I take deep solace in the community gathered within these pages.

Over the next year (and including this current issue), we begin a retrospective of the creative minds we have featured and the journey of *The Wayfarer*. In this issue, we look back on the poets.

Joy Harjo writes, "When I began to listen to poetry, it's when I began to listen to the stones, and I began to listen to what the clouds had to say, and I began to listen to others. And I think, most importantly for all of us, then you begin to learn to listen to the soul, the soul of yourself in here, which is also the soul of everyone else." Listen Deep.

Thank you for making this journey with us.

With Gratitude

[signature: L.M. Browning]

Leslie M. Browning, Founder & Editor-in-chief

(L.M.) Leslie M. Browning is a TEDx talker, photojournalist, and the award-winning author of twelve titles. In her writing, Browning explores the confluence of the natural landscape and the interior landscape. She holds an Associates degree in Philosophy from the University of London and a Liberal Bachelor or Arts from Harvard University focusing on English, Psychology, and Digital Media. In 2011, she founded Homebound Publications and its divisions, which has gone on to become a leading independent publisher in the country. She has served on the Board of the Independent Book Publisher's Association and is a Fellow with the International League of Conservation Writers. A vagabond-turned-homesteader, Browning is carving out a farm in the Berkshire mountains and holds a position at the press' main office in Northampton, MA. When not writing, or publishing the work of indie authors, she is roaming the mountains . . . which are ever-calling.

This issue is dedicated to Burt Bradley—
A Husband. A Father. A Mentor . . . A Poet.

WAYFARERS

RE-IMAGINING THE POSSIBLE

SPECIAL POETRY FEATURE

*Conversations with Poets
from The Wayfarer archive.*

ON POETRY AND BEING

AN EXPLORATION OF VERSE, FAITH AND POETRY'S PLACE IN THE HUSBANDRY OF THE SOUL

A CONVERSATION WITH
KRISTA TIPPETT HOST OF *ON BEING*
BY EDITOR-IN-CHIEF L.M. BROWNING
(ARCHIVE AUTUMN 2017 ISSUE)

Krista Tippett graduated from Brown University in 1983. After earning her degree, she traveled on a Fulbright scholarship to study at the University of Bonn in West Germany, where she wrote for *The New York Times* in divided Berlin as a freelance foreign correspondent.

Krista went on to earn a Masters of Divinity from Yale University in 1994. It is said that, while conducting a global oral-history project for the Collegeville Institute for Ecumenical and Cultural Research at St. John's Abbey of Collegeville, Minnesota, she began laying out the idea of what would go on to become her radio show, *On Being*.

Tippett would also go on to found "The Civil Conversations Project," which she has described as "an emergent approach to healing our fractured civic spaces". In 2008, her efforts in *Speaking of Faith-The Ecstatic Faith of Rumi* would win her a Peabody Award and then, in 2014, she would go on to win a National Humanities Medal at the White House for "thoughtfully delving into the mysteries of human existence."

Interwoven throughout each of these endeavors and indeed her faith itself has been poetry. I had the immense pleasure of sitting down with Krista this past summer to discuss the place poetry holds in her personal philosophy and where the roots of it run in her soul.

LESLIE: In many of your interviews, you like to start by giving the spiritual background of someone's life. And while the focus of our interview today is your use of poetry throughout the discourse of your work, I think we can both agree that spirituality and poetry are inherently alike. So, I'm going to start where you usually do, and ask you to just give a very brief spiritual background of your life.

KRISTA: Well, one thing I like about that question is that the answer changes over one's life. Over time, one thing that's happened is I've learned I have a very expansive understanding of the spiritual background in someone's life, which may be about religious formation or lack of religious formation. I think about spiritual life as *interior life*, and questions of meaning that live in us and that we follow.

I was actually just back in town—in my very small town in Oklahoma. . . there was a lot of religion in my background, that was hugely formative. Also, in this context of poetry, I think I was spiritually starved growing up of ideas and beautiful language, and something like poetry and literature.

So sometimes when people imagine that I have this great education, and this great grounding . . . I'm the opposite story. I'm the person who was never exposed to this stuff until I was really old, and then I kind of discovered it and couldn't believe how long it had taken.

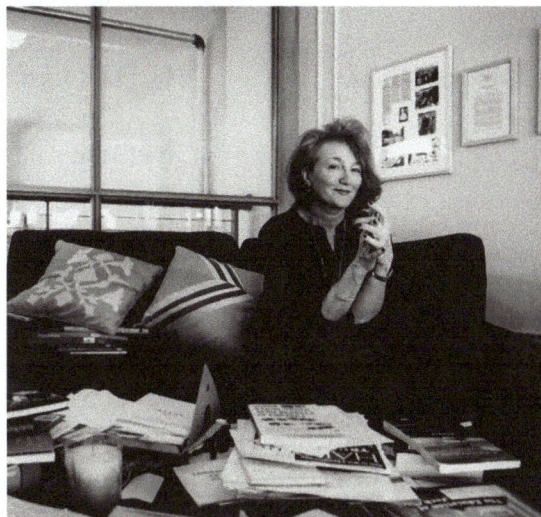

Speaking of Faith
Why Religion
Matters—
and How to
Talk About It
Krista Tippett

AUTHOR OF *BECOMING WISE*

"Krista Tippett has spent years using
her mind as a gentle but probing
research tool into the beautiful, perilous,
mysterious realm of the human soul."
—Elizabeth Gilbert, author of *Big Magic*

Einstein's God
Conversations
About Science &
the Human Spirit
Krista Tippett

NEW YORK TIMES BESTSELLER
AUTHOR OF *BECOMING WISE*

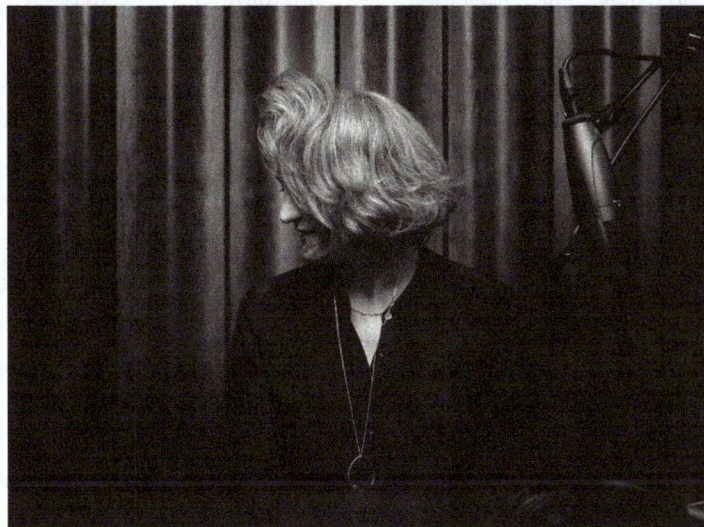

Becoming Wise
An Inquiry into
the Mystery and
Art of Living
Krista Tippett

NEW YORK TIMES BESTSELLER

LIE: What was your first experience with poetry?

KRISTA: Yeah, that's a good question. Again, I was not raised in a kind of literary atmosphere at all, or a home which had many books in it, or certainly not a home where people read poetry aloud.

I kind of think, it was growing up in the 60s and the 70s . . . For some reason, I remember E. E. Cummings. So maybe I saw some poetry that was playful. But I honestly don't think I read much poetry until I got to college. And I suppose the first poet who I felt like was a soul friend was Rilke . . . I discovered Rilke when I was living in Germany.

LESLIE: It's funny, you should say that. Rilke was the first poet I bonded with. I read, like so many people, *Letters to a Young Poet* and that was it. I was hooked on poetry.

KRISTA: Yeah.

LESLIE: I mean, like so many, that's kind of a very coming of age story for so many writers I think.

KRISTA: Yeah.

LESLIE: You gravitate towards poetry, the work of Mary Oliver and Wendell Berry and Marie Howe and Rumi and as you said, Rilke to name only a few, are interwoven throughout all of your books, and *On Being*.

Several figures you interview bring poetry into their responses, recognizing this, at one point you even assembled all such poems into episodes of *On Being*, the Poetry Project. What inner questions do you feel you're seeking the answers to when you sift through poetry?

KRISTA: Well, one thing I would say just is that I have gravitated more and more towards poetry, and that the show has gravitated more and more towards poetry. So, I think you would find this in the early years, but it's a very defining, recurring place now in my work, and in what I'm looking for in the world, and in what I'm listening for. I think, I wouldn't say that it's so much about a particular set of questions as it's about poetry's capacity to raise questions, and make observations using words and using forms

of language that give those questions and those observations a different kind of heft, and make them *ponderable.* I don't know if that's a word . . . [laughs]

LESLIE: Well we can make it a word. [Laughs]

KRISTA: Yeah. And I think that I've turned more towards poetry, as many people have, because the forms of speech that are more common are just so broken, and so bad for us. So, poetry, I wouldn't just say that poetry is an antidote to that, I would just say that we are rediscovering our need for language that gives us truth in a different way.

Right now, we have this kind of crisis of truth. But I actually think that the crisis is out on the surface. I think we've been moving towards it for a long time. And one of the ways we've been moving towards it is through this over-reliance on facts. And way too much confidence in what facts alone could ever convey.

LESLIE: Certainly.

KRISTA: And now, again, that's just out on the surface. I think a lot about a few things. I think a lot about Elizabeth Alexander saying to me that, "every line of a poem is not true."

In terms of another question, like "Did this really happen," or "Is it about you?" That every word and line of poem is not true, but that poetry gets at undergirding truths. And that's a really good way to talk about what we actually don't know how to discuss or put words around in our public life right now. We have no vocabulary for undergirding truths, to break through the competing facts and the thing I thought a lot about that helps me understand why poetry has become just that much more valuable is something David Whyte said to me just last year that, "poetry is language against which we have no distance." And right now, again, if I think about the different battles of our time, one of them is just this battle with defensive and offensive language. That's another way to understand how poetry cuts through that. And it still does, right? This is language also that makes you be silent, and just that is counter-cultural right now.

LESLIE: That couldn't be more true. Speaking of the current world climate, I just wanted to touch on a few of your memorable interviews with poets. You had a very poignant discussion with John O'Donohue two months before his death.

In that conversation, you discussed the importance of developing the inner landscape to keep us healthy in the midst of bleak surroundings and experiences. In the light of the current world climate, I can think of no more timely practice. What were some of the insights to tending to that inner landscape that you feel that you got from John, or have come to in your own time since? Where does poetry enter into the husbandry of the soul?

KRISTA: Well, in so many ways, right? There are the obvious ways, and then I think there are the less obvious ways. We were just talking about silence and stillness, and I think about years ago, I interviewed this individual whose mission it is to protect the last quiet places in the world, you know?

LESLIE: Wow.

KRISTA: Say things like, "Silence is a laboratory for the soul." Which is a lofty way to talk about the experience we've all had, and we know in the world around us. There's certain insights, and there's certain kinds of growth and learning that you just have to get quiet inside to make room for. And poetry does that.

You know, poetry is not easy. It's not easy. It's not entertaining. It can be soothing, but even when it's soothing it's asking something of you. Asking to soften up and open up ... And that also is a hallmark of inner-life too, there's a little bit of work involved.

LESLIE: Certainly.

KRISTA: Right? I remember having this conversation with Marie Howe and saying to her, "I sometimes feel like I have to be either wrecked enough or strong enough to read poetry." And she said, "Well it hurts a little bit going in, and we're so trained, culturally, to turn to things that don't hurt going in," right?

LESLIE: Certainly, yeah.

KRISTA: That make us feel better, or distract us. So, really, it's in so many ways both direct and indirect, it opens us for growth. And I think also, beauty, beautiful language. By which I don't necessarily mean sweet or frilly, you know what I mean?

LESLIE: Yeah.

KRISTA: Beautiful language can also be angular, and heavy, and hard. I think beauty is an *element*. I don't think poetry is optional. It holds some kind of reverence for beauty for inner-life.

LESLIE: I mean, right now, we're all starved for meaning, beauty, eloquence—those things that bring us to a moment of pause and awe, and awareness.

KRISTA: Yeah.

LESLIE: And I think poetry certainly aids in that. As we talked about earlier, when I was 26, I read two books that changed my life. And it was Rilke's *Letter to a Young Poet*, and his *Book of Hours*. After eight years of studying world religion longing to find a transcendent moment, I experienced it through poetry.

KRISTA: Yes.

LESLIE: In your book *Becoming Wise*, you say that Rilke became your friend across time and space, and that you were drawn, among many things, to his idea of living the questions.
Verse is interwoven into countless spiritual texts, the *Bible*, the *Quran*, the *Bhagavad Gita* . . .

KRISTA: Absolutely.

LESLIE: I believe that poetry shows its inherent sacredness when used to voice the ineffable. And, in *Speaking of Faith*, you say, "In many ways, religion becomes the same place in us that art comes from. The language of the human heart is poetry." Do you hold poetry collections alongside those sacred texts? Do you think that poetry has the capacity to guide the soul in the same way that spirituality and religion does?

KRISTA: I do. And I think that's such an important point that you're making. I mean, sure, we could have a really complex conversation about how poetry engenders, spiritualizes, and speaks to this part of us and comes out of this part of us ... But the truth is, as you also pointed out, all of the great spiritual traditions have poetry woven all the way through them. So, there you go. Another thought that I really hang onto, that I think about a lot, is . . . I once interviewed this great theologian of the prophetic tradition. This is somebody who's not a household name, but if anybody who has studied the prophets, the biblical prophets, who were social action figures and he said to me, "Prophets have always also been poets," that one of the ways prophets kind of broke through the cacophony of what was happening culturally is to speak in disarming language. That their language is powerful poetic language. And of course, if you read the speeches of Martin Luther King, Jr., right?

There's poetry in there, even while he's making these strong political points. So, yes, absolutely, somehow, poetry emerges from and speaks to the spiritual aspect of us in the most expansive sense of that language. But I also think it helps bring that into the light of day of our lives in the world. I think it's a source of nurture for continuing to live with the outer world and all of its complexity. And I think that's one reason that the election of 2016 turned out as it did. You've got this surge of people reading poetry and gathering to read poetry, and downloading poetry from the internet.

LESLIE: Certainly.

KRISTA: So it's never merely interior.

Leslie: Oh no. I just read an article asking, "Where are all the poets right now?" Because of all the protests and uprising since the election, and the call for that poetic voice that we had in former generations.

KRISTA: Yeah.

LESLIE: And most people don't realize that it's there, that we're here—we're screaming—but the media machine is louder.

KRISTA: Absolutely.

LESLIE: In closing, I reflect back to something you wrote in *Becoming Wise*. You say, "I've come to understand the cumulative dialogue of my work as a kind of cartography of wisdom about our emerging world." Taking the hundreds of intimate conversations you've had with contemporary poets of our day, and your gathered appreciation for poets of the past, have you distilled a set of mile-marker truths on your own personal map that poetry has taught you? I mean, looking back, is there something that stuck out, that poetry or a certain poet has taught you over your life? Like when you connected with Rilke, obviously that was a mile-marker truth on your inner-map. Can you speak to that particular one, or think of others that have come along?

KRISTA: Well, maybe kind of jumping off of what I just said, the conversation I had with Elizabeth Alexander, which was back in 2010, has just continued to be a real tethering point for me. One of the things we talked about is how poetry is a way to raise questions, which is important to me.

I think of Elizabeth Alexander, a couple of questions that she's raised by way of poetry that are just very present to me now, and I'm really working with them. It is this aspect of our project that we call the "Civil Conversations Project." These questions kind of epitomize everything that we've been talking about—about what is it that poetry does that other forms of language don't do.

So, there's a poem she wrote years ago, which ends with a question, "Are we not of interest to each other?"

I quote that probably in every speech I give about Civil Conversations. For the project, we've created a guide and it's in there, because it cuts through all of the very busy ways we have right now of talking past each other, and fighting with each other, and talking, but in fact not conversing, and not listening. And it's a question I wish I could just throw out into the halls of congress, and just throw at into gatherings as a new framing. We still do have really hard things to work on and talk about together. But, what if we let our coming together be framed by that kind of question, "Are we not of interest to each other?" What if we started there?

Then another question that she raised, actually, in her poem *Praise Song for the Day* at the first inauguration of Barack Obama, "What if love were the mightiest word?" That's just, it's not . . . I thought it was an audacious question to ask in a political moment. And I don't think it could be asked except in the form of poetry. And there it is. And to me, that's another question that if we let it roll around in our midst, if we let it affect the way we approach each other in the way we choose our words, the way we choose our fights, it would change us.

"Krista Tippett, radio host and author, for thoughtfully delving into the mysteries of human existence. On the air and in print, Ms. Tippett avoids easy answers, embracing complexity and inviting people of every background to join her conversation about faith, ethics, and moral wisdom." —President Obama | Photo by Mandel Ngania/AFP/Getty Images

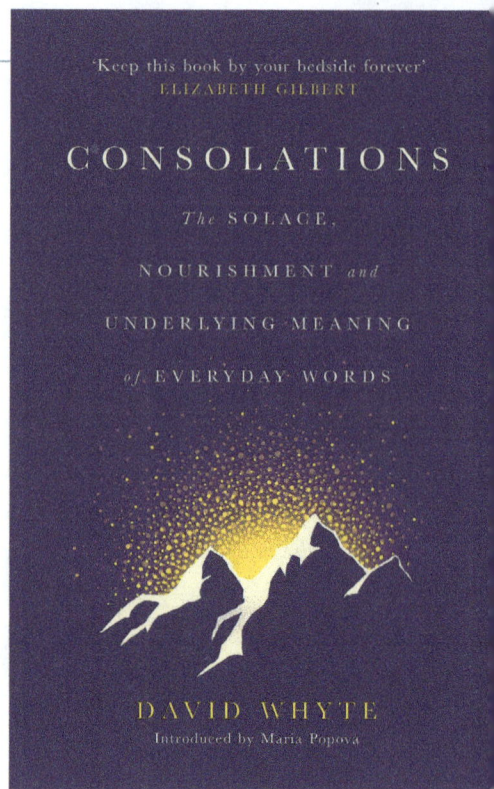

'Keep this book by your bedside forever'
ELIZABETH GILBERT

CONSOLATIONS

The SOLACE,
NOURISHMENT *and*
UNDERLYING MEANING
of EVERYDAY WORDS

DAVID WHYTE

Introduced by Maria Popova

THE INNER-FRONTIER

AN EXPLORATION OF VERSE, PSYCHE & SELF

A CONVERSATION WITH DAVID WHYTE
BY EDITOR-IN-CHIEF L.M. BROWNING

(ARCHIVE SPRING 2018 ISSUE)

Poet David Whyte grew up with a strong, imaginative influence from his Irish mother and found his true self while walking among the hills and valleys of his homeland. The author of eight books of poetry and four books of prose, David Whyte holds a degree in Marine Zoology, honorary degrees from Neumann College and Royal Roads University, and has traveled extensively, including living and working as a naturalist guide in the Galapagos Islands and leading anthropological and natural history expeditions in the Andes, Amazon and Himalaya. He brings this wealth of experience to his poetry, lectures and workshops.

His life as a poet has created a readership and listenership in three normally mutually exclusive areas: the literate world of readings that most poets inhabit, the psychological and theological worlds of philosophical enquiry and the world of vocation, work and organizational leadership.

An Associate Fellow at Said Business School at the University of Oxford, he is one of the few poets to take his perspectives on creativity into the field of organizational development, where he works with many European, American and international companies."

LESLIE: What was your first encounter with poetry?

DAVID: The first image I have in my mind and memory is of the silhouette of my mother, reciting to me in the Irish language, while sitting, at the foot of my bed against the light of a door always left ajar because there was no working light in my room. I felt in the gravitational pull of her voice, both completely present and in the presence of, while being introduced to a vast inherited world of which I knew I was a part.

LESLIE: When did you first know it was your path to be a poet?

DAVID: There were the first bodily intuitions, which had nothing to do with vocation, but with natural attraction, followed by a more serious confrontation of the inheritance of poetry. I happened to come across a large format copy of the Ancient Mariner by Coleridge, (One with the famous Dorée engravings) when I was nine years old. I remember having the book open on the kitchen floor while my mother worked around me and having an experience of both sheer terror and absolute fascination at one and the same time. Then at twelve, in the local library, I pulled down by my stretched fingertips, a collaboration of Thom Gunn and Ted Hughes, the reading of which felt literarily like being plucked up from the ground by a passing Hawk. That was the moment poetry really got its claws into me, an abduction, a kind of kidnapping of a growing identity that changed me forever. Though I stayed very serious through my years as a naturalist and world traveler, Poetry as a vocational path opened up to my imagination as a possibility only in my late twenties and then more seriously in my early thirties, when I first began to work with memorized poetry, my own and others, before live audiences.

LESLIE: You have said that, throughout your youth, you grew up with an imaginative influence from your Irish mother. In images and ideas what did she pass on to you at such a young age?

DAVID: The sense of a greater inheritance, another always present but unspoken context, a sense also of deep compassion for others and the struggle involved, of living even the most quotidien life. A lively, untrammeled sense of language, with laughter never very far away at the absurdity of it all.

LESLIE: Would you say she was your strongest influence?

DAVID: In one sense. In another I have had so many good influences in my life, from Latin Teachers to sea Captains! And then all those in the long lineage of poetry who have spoken to me and taught me, most especially William Wordsworth.

LESLIE: You've traveled extensively . . . the Galapagos Islands, the Andes, Amazon, and Himalaya to name a few. What places have imprinted themselves the deepest and how has that connection revealed itself in your work?

DAVID: Though I have been many, many places. The places most deeply imprinted are the places involved in my direct inheritance: the Yorkshire Moors and Dales and the Cumbrian Mountains of the North of England and in Ireland, the Atlantic shores of that land.

LESLIE: In addition to your poetic work, you lecture extensively on the philosophy of "Conversational Leadership." Could you tell us a little more about the idea of "Conversational Leadership?"

DAVID: Not fully in the space and time we have here! But essentially, in Conversational Leadership I am working with the timeless thresholds human beings have had to cross, whether they see themselves as leaders or no, in deepening any conversation. My next prose book looks at seven of these ancient and necessary ways of making the invitation that is necessary to any Leadership conversation.

LESLIE: In the work at present, we see upheaval and more and more we see leadership being replaced by self-interest. Could you see the philosophies of "Conversational Leadership" addressing these escalating challenges? In our last issue, we spoke with your fellow poet and colleague Krista Tippett regarding poet's place in the husbandry of the soul throughout heavy times, such as those we currently face as a global village. Would you agree that poetry speaks to and nourishes some part of us that isn't otherwise reached by religion and spirituality?

DAVID: The larger context, the perspective beyond what you have come to only think is a self, is what I address every day, through poetry, whether I am in Paris, France, or Paris, Texas, working with leaders and managers, literary hipsters, academics, or the dedicated religious, of all linguistic backgrounds, religious philosophies and cultures. Poetry has the great ability to address the deeper paths of the human psyche without setting off any inherited religious allergies... As I often say, poetry is language against which we have no defenses.

LESLIE: Indeed. Especially your work. Your poetry is layered with revelation as well as description. This is part of your signature as a poet. While there are numerous selections and offerings that come to mind when I think of your work, I will end with a selection of yours, in the poem, "Sweet Darkness" you write:

> When your eyes are tired
> the world is tired also.
>
> When your vision has gone,
> no part of the world can find you.
>
> Time to go into the dark
> where the night has eyes
> to recognize its own.

Can you tell us from where in your psyche this revelation sprung and what it speaks to?

DAVID: "Sweet Darkness" was written out of that very physical and almost breathless giving away, most human beings feel when they must let go of what seems most precious to them, not knowing how or when it will return, in what form or in what voice—that taking away of the light we experience walking through divorce or separation, through bereavement or through simply not recognizing the person looking back at us in the mirror. "Sweet Darkness" was begun in the early and darkest hours of the morning, in a kind of defiant praise of this difficult time of not knowing, a letter of invitation to embrace the beauty of the night and of the foundational human experience of not being able to see, as actually another horizon, and perhaps the only horizon out of which a truly new revelation can emerge. The last line cuts both ways of course, we ourselves have often helped to make everything and everyone around us, far too small, by our lack of faith in not knowing, by all the ways we are not holding the conversation with what as yet cannot be fully articulated. The essential work of poetry I might add!

LESLIE: In closing, can you tell us what you're working on now?

DAVID: In the world of works, am just finishing up a book of poetry 'The Bell and Blackbird" that I am very intrigued to recite from and work with for the next few years of my existence. When that is done and out in the world in mid-April I will return to my prose book on 'The Conversational Nature of Reality.' Titled *A Timeless Way: Seven Steps for Deepening any Conversation.*

On the interior edge, walking around in that body addressed only from the outside as David Whyte, I am practicing the ancient and difficult art of living more at the frontier between what I think is me and what I think is the world. It's the frontier that the writer writes at to write, the painter paints at to paint, and in the ultimate act of courage and bravery, the place from which to live, from the outside, what only looks like a most average life....

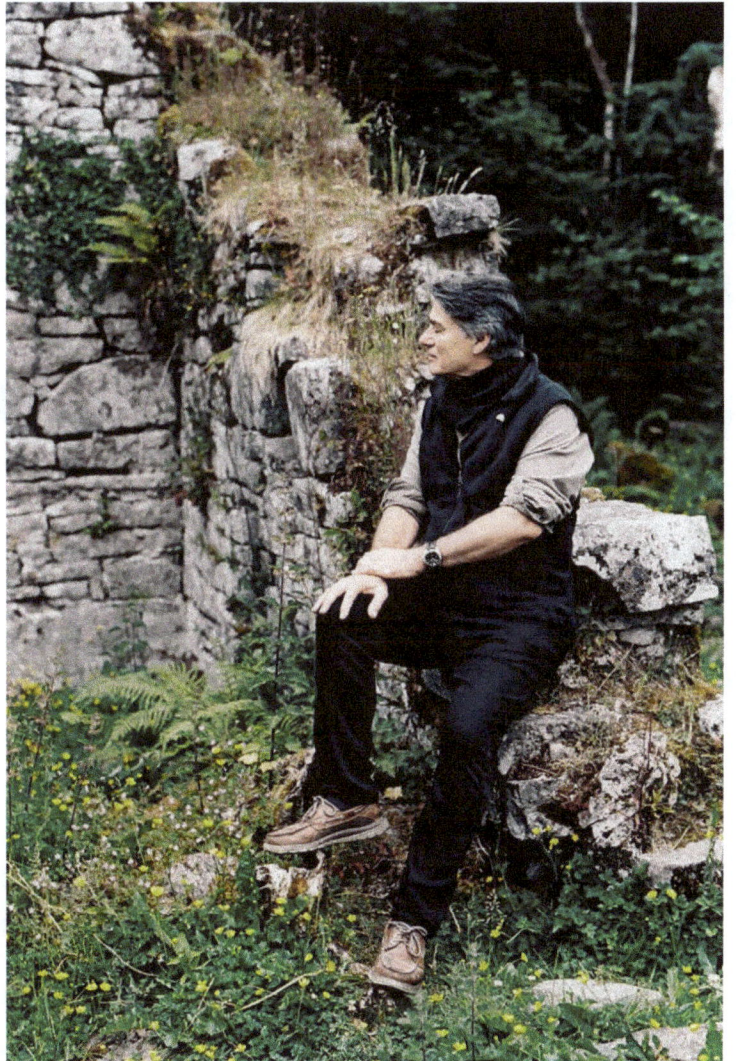

**Opening biography provided by the author. www.david-whyte.com | Photo at start of article Yorkshire Dale © Rob Bate | Author photo credit: © Michael Stadler

IN THE SHADOW OF SANDIA

EAST MEETS SOUTHWEST

AN INTERVIEW WITH THE POET
FRANK LARUE OWEN BY L.M. BROWNING

(ARCHIVE SPRING 2019 ISSUE)

THERE ARE CERTAIN PATH CROSSINGS that stay with you as fated moments—certain strangers who seem familiar to you—as though while walking through a crowded market, you brush sleeves with someone who knows you but doesn't know you. This was my experience meeting Frank LaRue Owen. When last we sat together, it was in the dusty high-desert of God's country. We sipped hot sake and ate sushi made with New Mexico Hatch green chile in a hidden away restaurant at the base of the Sandia Mountains in Albuquerque, New Mexico, and talked of the strange trails we poets find ourselves on in life. Sitting across from him, he is a man removed from the ordinary, insightful yet unpretentious, who is ever-shifting in dimension and depth. He is a poet, descendant of cowboys, and a fellow traveler.

Exploring the origins of his work, Frank LaRue Owen's poetry is influenced by dreams, the energies of landscape and the seasons, archetypal psychology, the Ch'an/Daoist hermit-poet tradition, and Zen living. He studied for a decade with a Zen woman who—inspired by Ch'an and Daoist tradition—blended silent illumination (meditation), dreamwork, mountain-and-forest spirituality ("landscape practice"), and poetics into a unified path. Owen also studied eco-literature and eco-poetry with the late Jack Collom, a poet and professor in the Jack Kerouac School of Disembodied Poetics at Naropa University in Boulder, Colorado. His first book of poetry, *The School of Soft-Attention*, was the winner of the 2017 Homebound Publications Poetry Prize. *Leslie: What would you consider your creative origin to be—what confluence of events came about to help you form your poetic voice?*

Frank: Some of the very first poetic language I ever encountered was the *Tao Te Ching* and the *I Ching*, the latter of which being an oracle from the ancient Chinese tradition. My mother studied the *I Ching* early in life as part of her Jungian studies and shared it with me in my pre-teen years. In addition to being among some of the oldest expressions of human literature, these works foster a means of thinking symbolically, poetically, oracularly.

On the heels of this, I came across a book in my father's study entitled *Black Elk Speaks*, which was already a classic when it fell into my hands. The visionary experiences of this Lakota holy man, and the mystical-poetic language Black Elk used to describe his experiences, were a formative source that shaped me as well. Additionally, Shunryu Suzuki's *Zen Mind, Beginner's Mind* set me on a search early on as a kid.

Putting something to paper myself as a fledgling poet, to translate my own experiences, started in early high school. This was before the internet, of course, so I frequented libraries. Alongside my own poetic experimentation, I studied various sources that supported this endeavour, from the writings of Jung to Joseph Campbell's *The Power of Myth*, an extended interview conducted by the journalist Bill Moyers. From that I was led to the poetic language of the *Bhagavad Gita* and *The Upanishads*, and this stoked an early interest in world poetry, mystical poetry, and nature poetry, which then led me to the Japanese poet Bashō.

Like so many of our ilk, I've also been inspired by the works of Mary Oliver, Gary Snyder, David Whyte, Hafiz, and Rumi. The poems of Joy Harjo, fellow Mississippian Natasha Trethewey, Joseph Stroud, Jim Harrison, and all of the female and male poets of the Chinese and Japanese tradition are never far away.

As for a confluence of events, I would have to say the real crossing of the bridge from being a lover of poetry to a writer of poetry, in earnest, is inseparable from crossing paths with certain teacher figures in my life. They installed a confidence for diving in.

Leslie: Speaking of teachers, you studied eco-literature and eco-poetry with the late Jack Collom, in the Jack Kerouac School of Disembodied Poetics at Naropa University in Boulder, Colorado, which was founded in 1974 by Allen Ginsberg and Anne Waldman. What did you take away from your time at Naropa in a creative sense?

Frank: Mindfulness, and coming into a firm allyship with one's own heart-mind, undergirds everything at Naropa, from the various psychology programs to the writing program. The main takeaway I received from Jack, in particular, was the practice of deep observation in creative work, on the one hand, and playfulness on the other. Jack was kind of a holy clown in my view, whose creative levity was contagious. He worked with people of all ages around poetry, including little kids in the Poets in Schools movement. Overall, though, what Naropa taught me creatively was permission to create.

Leslie: Beyond traditional learning spaces, we all have mentors who touch us deeply along our journey. You speak of a "Zen woman" your path converged with out in the mountains of New Mexico—a landscape of deep magic in and of itself. Would you mind telling us a little about this meeting and the impact this relationship had on your creative work?

Frank: Known as doña Río to some of us, Darion was a truly remarkable person who touched many lives in different ways. She was chameleon-like in her interests and in the methods she used in her guidance work with individuals and groups, which she loosely called "life path exploration". She would take on different qualities and emphasize different approaches depending upon who she was working with, and this included various methods from Asian spiritual traditions, Mesoamerican sources, wilderness rites of passage work, and Jungian psychological models.

Reflective of this, for example, in my first phase of knowing her (the early and mid-90s in Colorado), we worked almost exclusively with Zen practice; namely silent illumination meditation, meditation on phrases (known as huatou/wato in China and Japan), and frequent knee-to-knee interviews that Japanese tradition calls dokusan. When I look back on that time, I think she was just setting the stage for things to come, along with trying to help me become more of an ally to my own heart-mind.

Later on in the late 90s and 2000s, after a life detour on my part to D.C., and a move to New Mexico by her, at which time she became more hermetical, her work with me shifted. With a firm foundation of meditation having become second nature, the work became more focused on landscape and dreamscape, and poetics was a means of processing experiences with both. I made frequent cross-country trips each year to New Mexico to study this Southwestern "green chile Cowboy Zen" with her, including whole months at a time, and "the classroom", the "zendo", so to speak, was a mix of time in an adobe house in Santa Fe, time in the forests of the Pecos Wilderness, and time out in the desert.

Despite knowing her as well as I did, she remains a mysterious figure to me. She was very much a horse person, was constantly doing dreamwork throughout the day (because, in her own words, "We're never not dreaming"), but I only know small fragments about her life, which included her own experiences studying with Ch'an and Taoist teachers, and trips into southern Mexico to study with a curandera and a seer.

Leslie: You follow in her footsteps as a "mysterious figure." You seem a modern-day, reclusive, Zen hermit-poet more suited to the age of Ryōkan than that of this era. How do you see yourself within the current poetic landscape?

Frank: I definitely have a need and a leaning for solitude. It is how I refuel and solitary time is when I am afforded the potential to delve into the creative process. In general, I find many aspects of modernity overwhelming, if not downright insane, so there is a lot about the world I don't engage with. But, that said, I wouldn't call myself a recluse because I still enjoy being around people and have a commitment (at least for now) to stay engaged in the world and remain connected to community, such as it is.

I'm also not a true hermit by most people's idea of the term, but I do live a pretty solitary existence, and, at times, have emulated the lifestyle of certain early Ch'an poets who lived in urban settings, held day jobs, but stayed to themselves at night and went on mountain retreats as often as they could to focus on their poetry and Zen practice.

A lot of this may be a natural leaning for me, since even in my senior year of high school I avoided typical high school activities. I would come in from the day, drop my books, and head straight out into the forests behind my mother's house in North Carolina.

Being a solitary in recent years is also due to circumstance. From 1995 to 2005, I was very active out in the world. In fact, I was facilitating retreats along the themes of dreams, consciousness, contemplative practice, nature, and ecopsychology. However, in 2005, and especially in 2007 when doña Río died, I intentionally turned inward. Initially, grief was the motivator. But, then I began exploring the biographies of certain hermit-poets and felt an immediate affinity with how they had arranged their lives.

Some years I would put this exploration on the back burner and, for example, focus on relationship. Other years, my creative process has been the only thing for which I have held space. Both types of cycles have taught me a great deal.

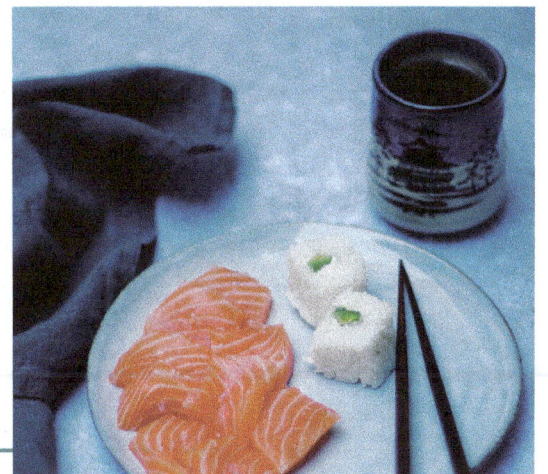

"As I age, living a slower pace becomes even more important to me; to connect with the land, to practice Zen, to explore ancestral energies, cultural streams, and heritage, and to write.

This year, I'm crossing into my 50s, and also clocking my fourteenth year of wandering down the same path I began walking with doña Río, spiritually and creatively. I have no idea where it is all going. As I age, living a slower pace becomes even more important to me; to connect with the land, to practice Zen, to explore ancestral energies, cultural streams, and heritage, and to write. But, yes, most days I feel like you could probably drop me in a Japanese forest or back behind a mesa in New Mexico, and I'd be okay.

Where this places me in the poetic landscape I'm not entirely certain. Perhaps one way of putting it is this. All poets are oriented to paying attention. They are attuned to the life around them. I am as well, but I'm also oriented to the life of nature, the inner life, and other non-obvious realities.

Leslie: Delving into your practice of holding space, tell us about your creative process.

Frank: My creative process is definitely a lived and living experience. Various natural images come to mind that express this. Climbing a mountain. Disappearing into a forest enveloped in clouds. A river that has its own particular flow but which also reflects, in some sense, what it encounters as it flows along.

At times, my creative process has felt like attending to a rather cosmic relationship; to what East Asian cultures call the Dao (Tao, The Way). As I say in the Preface of *The Temple of Warm Harmony,* "...'round and 'round the sun-like Dao." Sometimes that is what my creative process has felt like.

Lately, the working metaphor for my creative process has been riding a horse. Writing has begun to feel akin to saddling-up, heading out on a trail, and journeying beyond known trails into uncharted territories. In some cases, the "horse" is the horse of memory, taking me back into childhood, or into the multidimensional muscle memory and memory of the senses that gets registered when visiting a place.

I'm currently working on my third book, *Stirrup of the Sun & Moon,* which is tethered to experiences of memory of mind, dream, and place. My heart-mindstream is awash in a cascade of images, insights, and impressions, so my creative process has become one of registering these impressions, sifting through them as if panning for gold. A few of these kinds of poems have made prior appearances, such as "Quantum Travel" in *The School of Soft-Attention* (2018), but now I'm following the thread more closely where mindscape, dreamscape, and landscape touch.

Practically speaking, I wake up with my creative process every day because the moment I awake I am processing impressions from the dreamtime. So, notetaking, journaling, and trying to pull dream vignettes and fragments through the permeable membrane of consciousness that separates the dreaming and waking worlds is part of my daily course. That, and talking out loud to myself. [Laughs]

I live alone so I may even talk out loud to myself as a means of conjuring flashes of the dreaming mind so as to bring through the images that were experienced in a dream, or that are still fluttering about at the periphery of awareness in the dreaming body (which, of course, extends beyond the physical body). This activity is really rooted in the technique of active imagination from the Jungian tradition. It works well with dreams, it works well with poetry, and some day I hope to apply it to the realm of fiction.

Leslie: What do you think the role of the poet is in the current world climate?

Frank: We are living in a truly disturbing time. Not to oversimplify current conditions, or add unnecessary layers of lathered-up fear, but the energetic reality we are in strikes me as a battle of wills, conscience, and consciousness.

There are some whose consciousness is on a destructive footing. Destructive of earth. Destructive of societal, economic, and governmental norms. Others of us reject this on civic, environmental, and humanitarian grounds.

The poet in such times is what the role of the poet has always been: serving as a collective conscience (not holding our tongue about injustice, for example), but also reminding us all that, despite the presence of despots of delusion and dysfunction, that the numinous level of reality—of beauty, of grace, of healing, of sacred mystery—still exists, and will endure.

In this way, the poet can be a healer, a transmitter of perennial wisdom, and a culture of harmony rather than degradation and divisiveness. Indeed, as both conscience and purveyor of elevated consciousness, the poet can remind us all who we really are, individually and collectively. It seems to me we need both of these functions now more than ever.

Leslie. What words of hard-earned wisdom would you impart to those creative minds still seeking out their voice and getting ready to "saddle up" and head out onto the trail?

Frank: Become an apprentice to your deeper self. This includes one's dreams and the wise characters found therein. It also includes checking in with yourself multiple times during the day. Surface world technological distractions can be a real obstacle to such deeper attunement. There is a natural human wisdom inherent in the person that practices mindful attentiveness. Make it a practice.

Trust that one's own voice is linked to one's creative process, which has a life of its own. It has its own flow; you're just along for the ride. You can paddle and steer, but you can't push the river.

Trust that one's voice and creativity has a purpose that has its own seasons and rhythms. Live closely according to those rhythms. Live in attunement with the seasons of your creative life. Honor the fallow times just as much as the inspired and abundant times of creative harvest.

When it comes to creative writing, eject modernity's cold, lifeless notions of writing being mechanical and product focused. If you want to do writing like that, get a job in advertising.

I would also add, try holding the notion that writing (or any creative endeavour) is not an exclusively intellectual exercise. Try on the experience of writing as a full-bodied somatic experience including giving voice to hunches, impressions, 24/7 lucid dreaming, like picking up flavours and aromas from the ethers. Creativity can be a multidimensional experience involving senses beyond just the five we usually rely upon.

Held in this way, there is no such thing as writer's block. Even when you aren't actively writing, you realize you're working, or are 'being worked,' by the larger process; what I call "the poet's dreaming body" is actively working, observing, recording, seeing. Learning to trust in that feels related to trusting one's creative voice. Don't dismiss anything in your experience.

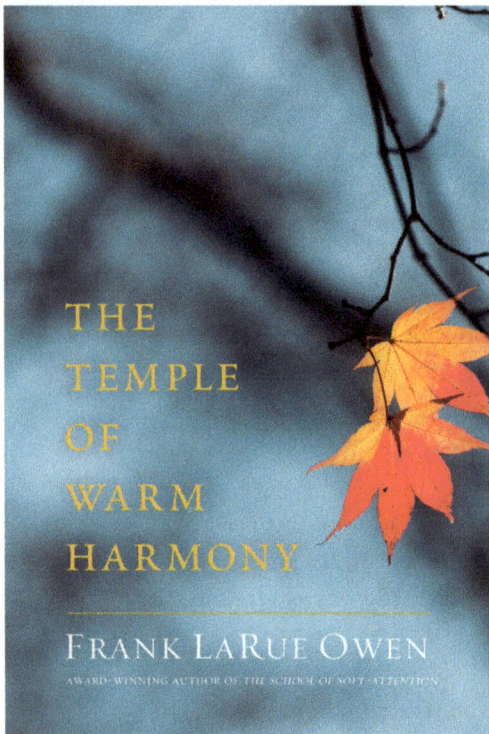

THE
TEMPLE
OF
WARM
HARMONY

FRANK LaRue OWEN

AWARD-WINNING AUTHOR OF THE SCHOOL OF SOFT-ATTENTION

THE BOUQUET OF THE LAST DIRECTION

by Frank LaRue Owen, *The School of Soft-Attention*

When the soul becomes unburdened
it's like a new saddle on a fresh horse.

Suddenly the trail feels right again,
and the strong horizon line in front of you as you turn
becomes its own form of soothing medicine.

Something of the sting and burn of the old poison may linger
but having crossed over from the Shadowlands
into new open territory, one can almost
pick up the scent of blooming flowers within.

You start to notice all the things you hadn't been
all because you'd been so bound up
with the echoes of losses and hauntings.

You know you're ready when ghosts
start chanting from the edge of your life:
Traveler! Good Traveler!
Your 'Crying for a Vision' Time is over.
Time to re-inhabit the Human World!

Then, the simplest of the ten thousand things
start to reach out to you to welcome you home again.

The Morningstar.
The blue sky with its utter completeness.
The serrated clouds coming over the rising pine-covered hills.
Even the food tastes better in the Land of the Great Eastern Sun.

You may find the wandering wild animal of your heart
is somehow more free to travel back through time...
...to pick back up with sources of beauty
and power you had put down.

And maybe, just maybe,
you'll see yourself now
through your childhood eyes
and you'll stand forgiven and realize
the magic you had then never left you;
you just forgot how to listen.

INSTRUCTIONS HANGING FROM A WEATHER-BEATEN BRANCH

by Frank LaRue Owen, *The Temple of Warm Harmony*

To illuminate The Way,
study the wayfarers of old.

Take up the Timeless Work
of untangling the soul.

Align heart-mind
with Nature's flow.

Journey into the dark
to mine the hidden gold.

When the Lantern-Lit Mind
abides in Silent Illumination,
the wayfarer's poems bear the mark
of the Great Transformation.

MOUNTAINWISE STOREHOUSE

by Frank LaRue Owen, *The Temple of Warm Harmony*

Ceaseless reminders.
Worldly imperfection.

People,
whole worlds,
out of harmony
with the Way.

Centuries of misalignment
leave spine-jolting ruts
in the road.

This is why
we go to the
mountains;
to remember
the Great Realignment
always available
to the supple-hearted.

A WILD VOICE AT LARGE

A CONVERSATION WITH CHRIS LA TRAY BY L.M. BROWNING

(ARCHIVE AUTUMN 2019 ISSUE)

As a lover of feral writers and voices calling from a solitary wild place, I cannot help but feel the pull towards the work of Chris La Tray. Of the books, currently stacked higgledy-piggledy atop my night stand, La Tray's *One-Sentence Journal: Short Poems and Essays from the World at Large*, is one—it is current sitting in-between the new collected/selected poetic works of Jim Harrison and the journals of John Muir. This offering was the winner of the 2018 Montana Book Award. It is also a finalist in two categories in the High Plains Book Awards: Best First Book and Best Book from an Indigenous Writer.

Leslie: Thank you for joining us, Chris. I often like to start at the beginning and as writers what would you consider your creative origin to be—what confluence of events came about to help you form your voice as a writer?

Chris: First, I love the word "confluence." It's a great river word. And there are actually two here, I think. One is the confluence of events that made me want to write in the first place. I was a big reader when I was young and gravitated toward fantasy: J.R.R. Tolkien of course; C.S. Lewis, Frank Herbert, and Robert E. Howard were big deals to me too. When I hit 7th/8th grade, my older cousin introduced me to *Dungeons and Dragons*, and I totally went head-over-heels for it. I think the storytelling aspect of the game combined with the existence of fiction that fueled it made me think, "Hey, I think I want to do this!" When I graduated 8th grade, my English teacher awarded me the reading award, which was a little blank journal. Inside she inscribed it as being a contribution toward "writing my first fantasy novel."

Which I did! I wrote a couple desk drawer fantasy novels, and they taught me how to finish stuff. Then I started freelancing for the local papers, some magazines, etc. At that time I was also writing crime/noir/pulp short stories and thinking about novels, but it seemed to me everything interesting was already being done, better than I could do, or just rehashed. My reading evolved, and my writing evolved with it. I don't think I realized I'd found my true voice until my book came out and people really started responding to it. That would be the second confluence, the act of putting it out into the world.

Leslie: Your first book, *One-Sentence Journal: Short Poems and Essays From the World At Large* won the 2018 Montana Book Award. Could you tell our readers the inspiration behind this work?

Chris: *One-Sentence Journal* isn't something I set out to write, really. I didn't agonize over how it might work or anything like that at all. I never even thought about it being a book until about ten minutes before it was one, heh. I'd been writing these single sentences pretty much every day for several years, without any plan for doing anything with them. It was just part of the writerly practice I was trying to be committed to; at the time I was working a job where I traveled a lot, and sometimes that was the only writing I could make time for. I'd also write little essays that I would post on my website about things I thought about, weird encounters I had, etc. Just short little vignettes.

I'd been reading Jim Harrison for several years, and I acquired a copy of the book *Braided Creek: A Conversation in Poetry* that he wrote with Ted Kooser. It is a collection of very short poems that Harrison and Kooser had been exchanging with each other via post card. When I read them, a little light went on over my head

ONE-SENTENCE
JOURNAL

SHORT POEMS AND ESSAYS FROM THE WORLD AT LARGE

CHRIS LA TRAY

about the sentences I'd been writing, that maybe, with a little reorganizing, they could be made into short poems. So I culled the lame sentences from the ones I liked best, tweaked them a bit, and it seemed to work. From there, it was a pretty short span from idea to book, almost an accident. But it worked out well.

I should also say I find myself more inspired for this kind of thing now than I was before. This work has swung a door wide open to the work of the old Japanese and Chinese hermit and wanderer poets that I really wasn't aware of. Like Bashō, who was doing these prose/poem hybrids—"haibun" is the form, which he essentially invented—more than 300 years ago. It's really blown my mind, feeling this kind of connection across centuries and cultures. It's wonderful.

Leslie: You are a member of the Little Shell Tribe of Chippewa Indians. While the tribe is recognized by the State of Montana, they currently are not Federally-recognized. This seems one of your most-passionate issues. Explain to our readers who may not be well-versed in the issue, what Federal recognition grants to a tribe and how this impacts the day to day life of the Little Shell people as well as other tribes throughout the country likewise without Federal recognition.

Chris: This is a big question, Leslie, akin to asking a sweaty evangelist, "What can you tell me about Jesus?" but I'll do my best to be brief. I should also point out that, depending on when this piece runs, we—the Little Shell people—might be headed to recognition, as the legislation is in place and attached to a big defense bill that pretty much has to pass before the end of September. So we might just be waiting for a signature (it's sickening to me, frankly, how this is going down: recognition via a defense bill for the nation that tried to wipe us out, our existence being signed into "approval" by the most loathsome of colonialist archetypes imaginable ... ugh).

But anyway. What Federal recognition will give us mostly is access to health services, housing services, and various other services available only to recognized tribes. It will enable us land (that we have to pay for, mind you) that will be held in trust by the government, that only we and the feds have jurisdiction over (a whopping 250 acres guaranteed, when there are thousands upon thousands of acres of unceded land north of the Missouri River that is ours). It will allow us to deal with the United States as a fellow sovereign nation, and grant us the ability to make laws and things that we feel are of benefit to our people. I know many people think all of a sudden the cash spigots get turned on. That is not the case at all.

Leslie: How does your Little Shell heritage affect your voice as a writer and your place as a Montanan?

Chris: Being Native inhabits everything I do. It always has. I didn't grow up on a reservation; we don't have one. That's part of not being recognized by the Feds. But I didn't even hear the words "Little Shell" until maybe ten years ago. It wasn't something I grew up with, I just knew we were "Chippewa" even though my father denied it. He denied being related to any other La Trays around

Montana, and there are a lot of them. This kind of trauma, and this denial—the results of a very calculated scattering of a band-based culture of close family ties and specific cultural attributes—is very common to Indian country. How? Why? That is what I'm writing about now. It's something I've been thinking hard about for the last few years and really focusing on. Sometimes it's hard.

Leslie: One cannot bring up Montana-based writers without conjuring to mind the late Jim Harrison. Your work seems to share a deep sense of connection with his work. Would you agree?

Chris: Absolutely. I don't know that my book would exist as it does without Harrison's influence. The people I've met because of a shared interest in his work is a long, wonderful list. The man had a wide reach, and still does.

Leslie: What have you taken away from Harrison's work? Are there other writers who have served as mentors along the path?

Chris: A thing I love about Harrison's work is that he didn't stick to one thing. He identified as a poet (and died, heroically, at his desk, pen in hand, writing a poem), but also wrote novels, novellas, essays, criticism ... whatever he wanted to. I love that. He was vocal in his opinions. He loved the natural world. He was surly but also had a big heart, from what I'm told by people who knew him well. That's not a bad legacy. I sat in a car with my father-in-law at the end of Harrison's driveway in Patagonia, Arizona, but couldn't screw up the courage—or rudeness, rather—to go knock. Not two months later he was dead. I wish I'd met him, but I don't regret my failure to approach. His last year or so was difficult, I know.

I'd be an asshole if I didn't mention James Lee Burke. Talk about a career, and talk about a true gentleman. He gets lumped in as a "mystery writer" but the man flat-out writes great literature. I've had the opportunity over the last few years to spend quite a bit of time in his company and I've learned a lot about how to deal with people, the industry, all of it, just by listening to him. I enjoy his company, and knowing him has made a big impact on my life. He lives full-time in the vicinity of Missoula now, and our community is the better for it.

I don't know that my list of influencers is so different from others who write the kind of stuff I do. Mary Oliver. Rachel Carson. Thoreau. Leopold. Barry Lopez. Contemporary writers like Robert Macfarlane and Robin Wall Kimmerer knock me out. They inspire me, but mentor? I don't know. I love the community I'm part of. They're the ones who lift me up and make me want to do good work. Some are names people recognize but many are ones that most won't. But they are all equal to me and I love them all.

Leslie: Finally, we always close this feature with the question, What do you view the role of the writer/artist to be in the current political climate? Given that you are a politically-active writer, I am deeply interested in your answer to this.

Chris: I know there are many writers who say they don't want to talk about their politics because they don't want to "alienate any of their readers." That just doesn't work for me. Art is how we fix things in the world, how we inspire people. Art for anything else is just bullshit commerce. The stakes are too damn high and there are too many things I care deeply about that can't defend themselves against the cancer that is this growth-at-all-costs economic model that is churning up the world. I try not to be a jerk about it, because we need to find ways to be civil to one another in the face of disagreement. But, for an example, you can't be any kind of person I want anything to do with while supporting separating families at the border and throwing them in cages. You can't agree to the prosecution of people who leave water in the desert in an effort to save lives. There is no argument in favor of either of those things, and the list of similar things that are happening is heartbreakingly long. We have let the soulless, inhumane, criminal activities of the super-wealthy become the status quo. There is no bliss in being ignorant of that. It's time we rectify that situation. If you don't like that, go ahead buy someone else's fucking book.

Follow Chris' work at: www.chrislatray.com | Instagram: @metischris | Twitter @metischris

Look for Chris' latest offering, *Descended from a Travel-Worn Satchel*

OUR ANGEL OF THE GET THROUGH

A CONVERSATION WITH ANDREA GIBSON BY L.M. BROWNING

I FIRST SAW ANDREA GIBSON (PRONOUNS: THEY/THEM/THEIR) PERFORM DURING THEIR *HEY GALAXY TOUR* AT BABEFEST—a feminist-focused festival—in Provincetown, MA. The headliner was Ani DiFranco. I remember sitting in my seat in the intimate theater waiting for DiFranco to come out when I read that Andrea Gibson would be the opening voice. I remember thinking to myself how odd it was for a poet to be the opening act for a musician. As a poet myself, I don't say this with judgment but rather with curiosity. When Andrea Gibson took the stage and began reciting their poetry, everything became clear. The poem recited: *Orlando* (touching on the Orlando shooting, which had happened only months before the evening in M.A.). There is little I can do to convey how powerful this poem is other than to say, in my humble opinion, that night the opening voice was even more captivating than the headliner, so instead I will simply encourage you to look up Gibson on YouTube, watch Orlando—and the rest of their videos—listen to it and then purchase it on iTunes so you can revisit it again. Gibson's most notable accolades being Four-time Denver Grand Slam Champion and Women of the World Poetry Slam champion 2008. Born in Calais, Maine, Gibson has lived in Boulder Colorado since 1999. Their poetry and activism primarily center on gender norms, politics, social reform, and the struggles LGBTQIA+ people face in today's society.

LESLIE: I'm going to dive right in . . . After seeing your first open-mic in Denver in 2000, you felt inspired to become a spoken word artist. What took place internally while you watched that open mic? What resonated so deeply with you?

ANDREA: I attended my first open mic in Boulder, Co, and my first poetry slam a few weeks later in Denver. I had written throughout my life but had such overwhelming stage fright I never imagined I would ever willingly read my poems aloud in front of an audience. Looking back now I realize that much of what drew me to the stage was how afraid I was of it. Fortunately (ha!) for me that fear has hardly subsided in 19 years of performing. My experience of attending poetry events these days is not very different than it was in the beginning. I don't know if it's possible to faint from goosebumps, but I feel on the verge of that consistently when listening to spoken word.

LESLIE: In *Lord of the Butterflies* you write, "Your name is a gift, you can return if it doesn't fit." In addition to "Andrea," you've also claimed the name "Andrew" and use gender-neutral pronouns, (specifically they/them/theirs). What were some of the mile- marker realizations along your process of defining yourself on the gender spectrum?

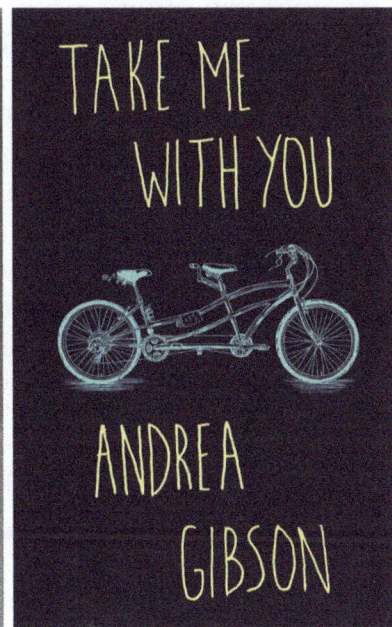

TAKE ME WITH YOU

ANDREA GIBSON

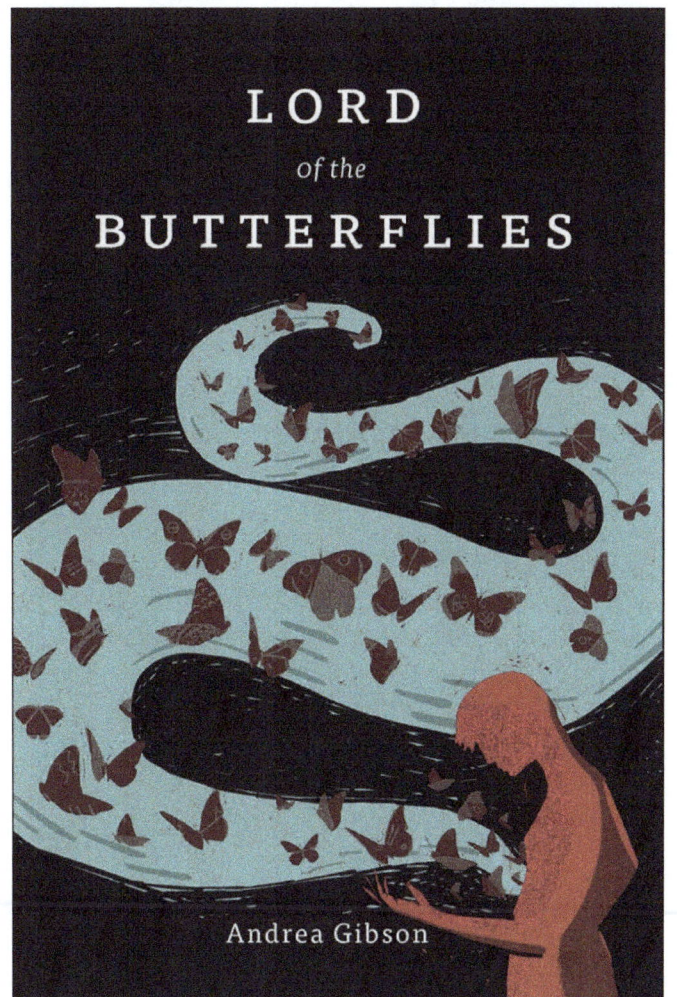

LORD of the BUTTERFLIES

Andrea Gibson

ANDREA: I was in touch with my gender long before I came to terms with my sexuality, and long before I had language to define myself. As a child I very simply didn't feel like a boy or a girl, and doubted I would ever grow up to feel like a woman or a man. In 2004 I heard the word "genderqueer" for the first time and immediately thought, "YES!" It wasn't until quite a few years later though that I started asking my intimate community to use non-binary (they/them/theirs) pronouns for me, and a couple of years later I began using them publicly and writing more consistently about my own gender journey. In regards to my name—I don't have much personal attachment to one, OR—maybe I just like having many names. Someone could ask 10 of my friends what they call me and there would be 10 different answers—Andrea, Andrew, Dre, Giba, Faye, Gib, Gibby, Sam, Andy, Pangee, Buttercup— yeah, I actually have a friend who calls me Buttercup. :)

LESLIE: Mental Illness—struggles with anxiety, depression, self-esteem, shame—all these inner-dynamics run like veins throughout your body of work. As one who likewise struggles with depression, PTSD and shame, one the most-resonate lines for me is:

> "I THINK THE HARDEST PEOPLE IN THE WORLD TO FORGIVE ARE THE PEOPLE WE ONCE WERE."

The unabashed authenticity with which you approach the pen unites all of us outliers, letting us know we are not alone. When did you decide that you were going to share those aspects of yourself? Was it a conscious choice to enter into this dialogue so wrought with taboo or were you simply being yourself?

ANDREA: People create their safety in different ways. I have a few friends who feel most safe when what they are experiencing internally is something they process internally. I'm the opposite. The more I share about what's happening in my emotional world, the more the tornado of my nervous system settles down. I don't doubt that that has been, in many ways, a response to trauma—my historical desire to have a voice that is heard, but it's one I feel good about honoring regardless. That said, as I've grown older, and have learned more and more to be the one who listens to myself, the one who shows up with softness when something deep inside of me starts screaming, I have less of a need to write to be heard as an individual, and more of a desire to show up creatively to a world harmed by silence. As you touch on above-- there is so much we have in common, and reminders that we are not alone can be life saving. Those reminders have certainly saved my life many many times.

LESLIE: When you recite a poem, your voice reverts with rhythmic, raging, raw rhymes. Each time you perform, you seem to not be reciting the poem but living it. When I gave a TED Talk on my own reality with mental illness, I felt like a streaker on stage—naked—only it was being recorded for posterity. The level of vulnerability was both terrifying and transcendent. Do you find it emotionally draining to give so much of yourself in every book, every performance? How do you refill yourself?

ANDREA: I most often find writing and performing energizing. I feel more alive while doing both than I do at almost any other time in my life lately. But there are some poems and some topics that leave me feeling more naked than others. For example, I have chronic Lyme disease, and speaking to that on stage specifically is something that I can't always do. When I started diving into the why of that I soon recognized that it's, in large part, because of the tenderness of my audiences. I feel most vulnerable when I can feel people worrying about me and when I speak to my health (what I perceive as) worry sometimes permeates the room. It's one of the places where I've been calling myself to be braver and to show up more courageously to my discomfort.

LESLIE: In "Angels of the Get-Through," you write,

...I AM ALREADY BUILDING THE MUSEUM

FOR EVERY TREASURE YOU UNEARTH

IN THE ROCK BOTTOM

HOLY VULNERABLE CLIFF GOD MASON,

HEART HEAVIER THAN ALL THE BRICKS

SAY THIS IS WHAT THE PAIN MADE OF YOU

AN OPEN OPEN OPEN ROAD AN AVALANCHE OF FEEL IT ALL

DON'T EVER LET ANYONE TELL YOU, YOU ARE TOO MUCH

OR IT HAS BEEN TOO LONG...

Is your creative process an excavation of rock-bottom? ...Is it the alchemy of transcending this life's pains into something of beauty? From what mental place do you usually take up the pen?

ANDREA: When I look at my life I don't see many absolute facts. Nor do I see many absolute truths. My life is what I call it and the more I have called it beautiful the more beautiful it has become. What I have called my biggest wounds have very often been my biggest blessings, because of where they led me, and because of how often they further opened my heart. I don't want to say any of this flippantly and without respect for how real this hurting world's walls are in relation to how possible it is to see the light in any given moment. But I have needed, for my own sanity, to find that light in every instant I possibly could, and that is most often where I write from, though it is not the only place. ...I'll say one of the other primary places I speak from is rooted in the belief that even when the truth isn't hopeful the telling of it is.

LESLIE: Have you ever written a poem that you were afraid to share? ...have you ever said to yourself, no, this is too intimate; I don't think I can share this one?

ANDREA: Yes. But there was a "yet" on the end of the sentence. "I don't think I can share this one yet." And hopefully soon, I will.

LESLIE: Finally, the first time I saw you perform was at Babefest in Provincetown. You opened for Ani DiFranco. I remember sitting in the audience awestruck as you performed "Orlando" –brought to tears as you kept going, verse by verse, striking the chords of my soul with each word.

"...PEOPLE OUTSIDE PUSHING BANDANNAS
INTO BULLET WOUNDS.
IT'S TRUE, WHAT THEY SAY
ABOUT THE GAYS BEING SO FASHIONABLE.
THEIR GHOSTS NEVER GO OUT OF STYLE.
EVEN LIFE, IT'S LIKE FUNERAL PRACTICE.
HALF OF US ARE ALREADY DEAD
TO OUR FAMILIES BEFORE WE DIE.
HALF OF US ON OUR KNEES TRYING
TO CRAWL INTO THE FAMILY PHOTO..."

LESLIE: What do you view the role of the poet/artist to be in the current political climate?

ANDREA: To inspire an untamable sense of urgency in regards to active boot-laced compassion. To actively imagine a better world and to write it down so that others might imagine it as well. To destroy the myth of our collective powerlessness. To create beauty where there isn't yet beauty. To remind people they are not alone. To un-war our relationships to each other and ourselves.

COLUMNS

"To be yourself in a world that is constantly trying to make you something else is the greatest accomplishment."
–Ralph Waldo Emerson

*"If you agree with me, I may yet be wrong,
but if the elm tree says the same thing, I know I am right."*
–Emerson

———

HEALING TREES

THE ENVIRONMENTAL COLUMN BY GAIL COLLINS-RANADIVE

Thirty years ago, I found myself facing a life-threatening illness that landed me at Walter Reed Medical Center for a full month. While the first few days of being tethered to an intravenous tube sewn into the top of my hand are mostly a blur, I can still clearly see a little tree standing by itself out in the courtyard beyond the hospital window.

I wasn't quite sure how I'd ended up where I was or what would happen to me next, but I did know in my bones that, as long as I could see that tree, I'd be okay. To this day I don't know how I managed the presence of mind and mustered the courage to seek permission to turn my bed to face the window instead of the ward. I just knew that I had to. Never mind that, unlike in civilian hospitals where staff made up patients' beds daily, you made your own bed in a military hospital. And that meant that the charge nurse came through the ward before dawn and kicked the foot of each bed to wake up its occupant so that the beds were made before breakfast. I made sure I was awake well before that kick to where my head now was, but from where I could see 'my tree.'

What was that all about? Back then, when my body was broken, my mind mushy, and the light of my spirit all but gone out, I would have been hard-put to explain it. Rather, it was simply the deepest knowing I'd experienced up to that point in my life: a knowing that my very life depended upon.

No wonder that a dozen years later, during another potentially serious health crisis when I couldn't reach the doctor's office that had left an alarming message on my home answering machine, I sought solace in a nearby park, where live oaks dripped with moss along the walking path. But this time, as I sat on a low-slung limb asking for grounding and guidance, I became upset instead of centered. At the time I was serving an interim congregation in coastal South Carolina that maintained a church building built during the American Revolution that had survived the Civil War. Members were deeply mindful of the legacy they carried forward with their talents and treasure; their dedication assured it would transcend their personal futures.

As I desperately tried to believe that the tree I was clinging to would go on long after me no matter how much time I had remaining, it hit me hard: this was no longer a given, with humans systematically destroying so many life-supporting ecosystems through centuries of exploitation and pollution. What were we doing?! Even the controversial story of the 'taking' boy growing to manhood in *The Giving Tree* made it clear that nature has limits.

We have long known that the earth's trees produce the oxygen that makes human and other life possible. Plus, they remove pollution from the air, prevent erosion of the soil, concentrate protein into the fruits and nuts that enable our high metabolism. Yet we have clear-cut forests for farming, ranching, mining, and making space for human needs and wants. In fact, we're now in the Anthropocene Age, the era in which human domination is driving other species extinct and changing the climate in ways that threaten our own existence.

Yes, ours is still a young species, but surely we are old enough to know better than to keep disrupting and destroying the natural world upon which our own lives depend! In fact our indigenous neighbors have long practiced an ethic of reverence, respect, and reciprocity towards nature. Even the dominating culture of our nation has also had its poets and activists on behalf of the natural world, from Ralph Waldo Emerson to John Muir, Henry David Thoreau to Edward Abbey, David Brower to Terry Tempest Williams, to name but a few.

And today planting trees has become a global effort to draw down the carbon that humans have put into the atmosphere; for instance, Homebound Publications has partnered with One Tree Planted to plant a tree for each book sold through their store. But major polluting corporations have also seized upon tree planting as a way to offset their carbon footprint without stopping their carbon emissions. They are grabbing huge tracks of land and displacing the local farmers, ranchers, herders, and hunters as they 'greenwash' their corporate image. Never mind that the tree saplings planted today will take decades to mature enough to remove the carbon being emitted today!

Alice Walker once wrote: "I knew that if I cut a tree my arm would bleed." Yet ironically, when we humans do bleed, or become ill, or suffer chronic ailments, trees provide the medicines that help us heal. Plus, they provide a remedy 'for what ails us' emotionally and spiritually as well as physically. As Diana Beresford-Kroeger, world-recognized botanist and medical biochemist, shares in *To Speak for the Trees,* "We

now know that the alpha-and beta-pinenes produced by the forest and released into the air are absorbed by your body and affect your brain through your immune system, uplifting your mood and allowing your imagination and creativity bloom." She also proved that "trees possess all the same chemicals we have in our brains and even have all the component parts necessary to have a mind or consciousness...and thus can listen and think and perhaps even dream."

Recently, during a year of relentless heath issues framed by pandemic and political crises, I sought comfort on my Las Vegas patio where I could be with a specific tree. With sweatshirt hood pulled up over my head to protect the pressure dressing on grafts for skin cancer, I felt as infirm as the tree I stared at. One whole section of it looked dead. Yet the rest of it still put out leaves that dance in the wild desert wind and provide some protective shade from the brutal desert sun. I've managed to keep my homeowner's association from cutting it down for the thirteen years I've lived here.

Afterall, its barren branches blossom with a variety of birds that then I can see instead of just hear. And even though not fully functional, this tree's other limb of leaves that become maroon-brown in the fall still faithfully serves the same life force that flows through me. If it could manage to hang on, how can I not stay engaged in the life/work that is mine to do, regardless of attention-demanding ailments?

Yet like many who have survived the still active pandemic, I now feel broken and vulnerable, and may never be the same again. Crossing my stone landscaped yard, I reach out to touch the damaged tree. While neither of us can fend off the ravages of wind, sun, and fate forever, maybe we can heal each other enough to keep on keeping on.

From the tree's top, a tiny feather floats down in a flutter of hope.

Gail Collins-Ranadive, MA, MFA, MDIV, is the author of 9 published books, 5 through Homebound that include *Chewing Sand, Nature's Calling, A Fistful of Stars, Dinosaur Dreaming, Inner Canyon, Where Deep Time Meets Sacred Space* and the forthcoming: *Light Year; A Seasonal Guide for Eco-Spiritual Growth.* She also sponsors Homebound's Prism Prize for Climate Literature.

"Our relationship with the natural world has existed long before our consciousness."
–David K. Leff

FOREST AND PARK
THE NATURE OF POETRY, THE POETRY OF NATURE
THE LIFE & THE ARTS COLUMN BY ERIC D. LEHMAN

A few years ago, at the inauguration of David K. Leff as the poet laureate of the New England Trail, I chatted with members of the Connecticut Forest and Park Association over wine and cookies. Outside a fearful storm blew rain against the building in sheets, making a dark night even darker. The nature-themed poetry by David and other poets inside had been sad, funny, and touching in turns, and seemed as natural to me as breathing. I had grown up enjoying the literature of travel and nature in magazines like this one, and assumed everyone felt the deep and enduring connections between the two. However, I found out during the conversation that many of the nature lovers in the room did not necessarily see that relationship. "I never listened to nature poetry before," one told me, seriously and sadly.

As a teacher of literature, it was a tough thing for me to parse out. Wasn't nature one of the big themes? Hadn't we all been forced to read Emerson or Frost in high school English class? But then, I got to thinking, there have been countless humans in every culture that have lived in, experienced, and cherished nature without reading books about it. One could walk in the woods without loving to read other peoples' experiences doing the same. One could appreciate the battle of a junco and a blue jay without wanting to put it into words.

And the opposite was also true. There are plenty of lovers of literature who do not think of "nature literature" when they go to the bookstore. Those who are aware that it is a "genre," may be unfamiliar with it except for the fact that they once saw *Walden* in a bookstore. What's more, actual experts in literature may think of it as a "lesser" genre, suitable for the Romantics and environmentalists, but otherwise not part of the "serious" curriculum.

This second problem is easier to deal with. After all, genre itself is a mere convenience. Authors write about their own concerns, and if one of these concerns is nature, then we too often shove their work into that cubbyhole with a winter jacket and Nikon camera. Sometimes it stays there for a hundred years or more. This cubby-holing of publishers, bookstores, and even readers' preferences prevents access rather than grants it. We must think of books like *The Snow Leopard* by Peter Matthiessen or *Pilgrim at Tinker Creek* by Annie Dillard not as "nature literature" but as literature. Away with the tyranny of targeted marketing! Welcome the gregarious chaos of the dollar-book table at the local library sale, where anything can happen. We must break down the barriers between "genres"

and return (or move forward) to a time when nature literature is not on one shelf on the back wall of the giant box store, but where it should be—amongst its fellows in the great jumble of ideas and stories that makes up our culture.

The first problem, though, was more serious, and made me think deeply about what nature writing really gives to the world, why this mediation was necessary. Wasn't a direct connection between person and natural world best? After all, as David Leff points out in *New England Nature*, "Our relationship with the natural world has existed long before our consciousness." So, what does the filtering of consciousness through language bring to the table that watching eagles on a sunny day on top of a mountain does not?

The answer may lie in the changing relationship we have with nature. A person at the dawn of the agricultural revolution ten thousand years ago would have felt differently about standing on that mountain than we do today. Their literature, filtered down to us from Mesopotamia and Egypt and India, is rarely one of personal epiphany or peaceful meditation or romantic description – the sort of relationships we might have today. They mostly speak of the struggle against nature, of the dark, forbidding mountains, of nature as a metaphor for religious beliefs. They speak of controlling nature through agriculture, through pushing back the forests, the tigers, and the floods. Gilgamesh tames the countryside; the Pharoah keeps the river flowing; the emperor of China builds a wall against the wilderness. The enclosed Garden of Eden is the paradise, not the frightening wilderness beyond.

Since the beginning of the industrial revolution, nature has become less and less something to be conquered, and more and more something to save. "The world is too much with us," William Wordsworth shouts as early as the 1790s. Wilderness shrinks into national parks, becoming small, tangled islands in the midst of organized, civilized lands. Thoreau's statement, "In wildness is the preservation of the world," would have been unthinkable to someone a thousand (or even a hundred) years earlier. Pleas to rescue something that is dying have become perennial, as have reflections on our loss of connection to the natural world (what percentage of Americans regularly hunt animals for food or till their fields to survive?). The last two hundred years have required new ethics, new ideas, and, of course, new literature.

In this way, we can see how literature processes and manages our feelings and ideas. It provides, over and over again, new languages for us to speak about our concerns. Even those who have never read a single line of "nature writing" will create the language to speak about their experience, to pass it to others, their children, their friends, or even themselves, late at night in a quiet hour of reflection. And in doing so, they are writing, even in a transitory verbal or internal way, the newest human language of what we call nature.

We might go even farther than that. We might even say that verse, story, and description transliterate the secret languages of the natural world into our human languages, into consciousness itself. If we can give people voices, why not give them to badgers, to sycamores, to rivers? We can explain, through word choice and metaphor, can be interpreters of the winter rustle of the dry marsh reeds or the summer song of a white-throated sparrow. We can, like the Lorax, speak for the trees.

In this way, literature is something shared, between human and nature, between voice and voice, between past and future. It may be that no work of literature will ever approach an actual walk in the woods. But without it, we might be walking alone.

Eric D. Lehman teaches creative writing and literature at the University of Bridgeport and his work has been published in dozens of journals and magazines. He is the author of fifteen books, including *Afoot in Connecticut, Homegrown Terror: Benedict Arnold and the Burning of New London,* and *The Quotable New Englander*. His novella *Shadows of Paris* was a finalist for the Connecticut Book Award and won a silver medal in romance from the *Foreword Review*. Look for his new novel *9 Lupine Road: A Supernatural Tale on the Tracks of Kerouac*.

INNER CLIMATE CHANGE

SPIRITUALITY IN THE AGE OF LONELINESS

—

THE CONTEMPLATIVE COLUMN BY THEODORE RICHARDS

I'm on the bus, in a crowd but somehow feeling lonely. We are heading north, along Lakeshore Drive, past Lake Michigan, its waves shimmering in the sunlight, waterfowl dancing along its edge. No one notices. Everyone is staring down at a device, existing in some other, personalized, curated, disembodied, individualized world. It's a world in which each is simultaneously consumer and product. It is the world crafted by a system, a worldview, called capitalism. In this world, each of us is ultimately alone.

I. THE RELEVANCE OF SPIRITUALITY TODAY

*The question we all have is not so much about what happens to
us after we die but whether or not we are alone in the Universe.
If we are alone, no afterlife would be worth much; for me, even
a blink of an eye with the possibility of true communion with
others would be preferable to such an eternity.*
–The Great Reimagining:
Spirituality in an Age of Apocalypse

How can we all be so connected and yet feel so alone? Is it possible that
the promise of a global village through techno-capitalism was a lie—the
Manichaean dream turned nightmare? I cannot help but think that there
must be something more to re-discovering a connection than a phone, that
this civilization is in need of some sort of spiritual re-awakening.

But is there a role for spiritual practice in the modern world? Are the old
traditions even relevant? In an age in which are institutions are collapsing,
in which radical political action is called for, isn't it a little self-indulgent to
focus on spiritual stuff? The answer is, well, maybe. It depends.

Most of what passes for spiritual practice today is what I will refer to as
capitalist spirituality—spiritual practices that offer personal, individual
salvation or happiness. And these practices are a little indulgent. It's about
stuff we can buy—modern indulgences—to enhance our individual lives.
That's because such spiritual approaches generally tend to be rooted in an
individualistic worldview—that is, the worldview of capitalism.

But wait, you might object, aren't these traditions rooted in ancient wisdom
that predates capitalism? This is true. But that often has little to do with
how a tradition is practiced in today's world. For a spiritual tradition is
always rooted in a deep and unspoken cosmology. And while we are now
privy to a wider array of traditional spiritual practices than ever before, the
way we approach them is profoundly limited by the constricted worldview
of capitalism, a worldview that teaches us that we are fundamentally alone,
responsible for our own successes and failures—our own salvation. It is no
wonder that as more and more Americans practice yoga or mindfulness, we
also consume more and more.

Spiritual practices, even if they originated in a cultural context that would
offer a more interconnected and relational sense of self, often only reinforce
the individualism of the capitalist worldview.

I am going to argue that the spirituality's fundamental task at this moment in history is to offer an antidote to loneliness. To be clear, I am not talking about the loneliness that results from merely being alone too much or from not having enough friends. This is part of it—a consequence of a deeper and broader loneliness. A cosmic loneliness.

To begin, the problem of loneliness is a delusion, albeit a powerful one. To understand how we get there, we must understand how human beings create our sense of self, community, and world. This is called a cosmology or worldview. And it is expressed in every culture through symbol and story. For millennia, human cultures around the world created myriad unique worlds through the stories they told. In each case, the human was understood as a part of a community, and a part of a broader ecological web.

But in the Modern world, a new story emerged. The human was considered to be primarily an individual, acting out of self-interest. Great divisions were made between the saved and the damned. Colonialism, The Protestant Reformation, and the rise of capitalism all contributed to these views. What's been lost in all this is the fundamental purpose of spiritual practice—to cultivate and embody a story that allows for us to find our place in relationship to one another, to the cosmos.

II: FROM CRISES TO CRISIS

"Totalitarian movements are mass organizations of atomized, isolated individuals."
–Hannah Arendt, The Origins of Totalitarianism

It is impossible to avoid the immensity of the climate crisis. Because its scope is global, and its threat is existential, it feels like the climate crisis is the greatest challenge humanity has ever faced.

At the same time, our species seems to be threatened by myriad crises: fascism is spreading from The United States to Europe to India to South America; economic disparities are increasing; geopolitical instability has led to migrant crises at the southern borders of both North America and Europe. I could go on.

But it would be a mistake to look at all these events as separate and disconnected. Our economic system, capitalism, requires constant, infinite growth. Constant, infinite growth on a planet with limited resources is leading to both economic inequality and to the climate crisis. No new technology can save us if we cannot deal with our consumption addiction. The migrant crisis is also a problem of climate. Across the globe, from Central America to the Sahel to the Middle East to India, there is a band of nations dealing with depleting resources, shrinking water supplies, and geopolitical instability. In many ways, these are climate refugees.

And all of this instability has led to the proliferation of fascist movements across the globe.

While it may seem like these are all different crises—indeed, there are times when the political discourse would suggest that the concerns of, say, the environment are at odds with justice for oppressed peoples—by taking a step back we can see that we are actually seeing a single, global crisis.

A crisis of story.

How was it possible for me to feel alone on that bus, in a crowd of people, next to a huge body of water teaming with life? It has little to do, obviously, with proximity to other people, or even access to nature. It's all about the story we are telling about who we are. For a cosmology, a worldview, is brought to life not by information about our world, but by a story we tell. And the story of our civilization is the story of individualism and separation. This is because capitalism requires us to believe that we are fundamentally alone, acting merely as individuals rather than as members of a community. How else could the system of global slavery been enacted but with a story that described some groups as less than human? How else could we destroy the biosphere but with a story that tells us we are separate from nature?

And if we don't feel alone, we won't keep buying what they are selling.

How was it possible for me to feel alone on that bus, in a crowd of people, next to a huge body of water teaming with life? It has little to do, obviously, with proximity to other people, or even access to nature. It's all about the story we are telling about who we are.

III: THE INNER CLIMATE

Whoever you are, no matter how lonely,
the world offers itself to your imagination,
calls to you like the wild geese, harsh and exciting —
over and over announcing your place
in the family of things.
–Mary Oliver, "The Wild Geese"

Our world isn't merely interconnected from crisis to crisis. The inner and the outer are also inextricably linked. Among the most pervasive—and problematic—of the myths that capitalism produces is the notion that our inner lives are somehow separate from the social and political factors that shape our world.

But that feeling of loneliness, our interior ecology, is not separate from the external conditions. The story that separates us from one another leads not only to climate crisis and fascism, it also has led to an epidemic of loneliness. The mass shooter proliferates in the age of mass extinction and mass incarceration. The opioid addict and the pill popping soccer mom are both looking for the same thing—a sense of place in the world.

If our worldview is made up of stories, then the collapse of those stories is experienced as the end of the world— an apocalypse. This is what was happening among the Israelite people when the apocalyptic tradition came about. Confronted with the global military power of Rome and economic pressures that upended their traditional ways of life, the Israelites saw their culture unraveling. The Hellenistic culture of the eastern Roman Empire was replacing the traditional Israelite worldview.

The genius of the apocalyptic tradition wasn't found in any predictions of the end of the world; it was found the visions of what might lie on the other side, when a new story and a new worldview emerges. Indeed, apocalypse means "unveiling." This was the vision of Jesus in the gospels, the "Kingdom" of a world in which the old values no longer applied.

Our situation today is no less apocalyptic, perhaps more so, than in Jesus' time. This isn't just about climate change. The individualism of the capitalist worldview has reached its nadir—absolute, cosmic loneliness. This is the loneliness of the mass shooter and the fascist who want to destroy a world that no longer feels like home, the loneliness of the addict and the corporate CEO who want to consume a world to replace a lost sense of self.

But it is important to note that this worldview—which, like all worldviews, feels so natural that it's just common sense—is an anomaly in human history. If modern home sapiens have been around for about 200,000 years, the modern capitalist worldview has only been a mere blip. For most of our history, human beings have created stories of belonging and relationship. This is how we survived. It isn't merely our big brains—indeed, those can build bombs that destroy us all. It's our ability to create community and belonging through symbol and story that allowed us to thrive. The human, without the sharp teeth of the lion or the speed of the gazelle, needed cooperation to survive.

And so, the old stories, and all the spiritual practices brought forth through them, were fundamentally narratives of belonging and relationship. When our ancestors drew pictures of the animals they hunted on the walls of the cave, they understood that this was their kin.

Later, complex philosophical systems arose to reinforce the relationships upon which we all depend. Throughout Africa, for example, individual personhood is understood to have meaning only in the context of other people. This concept, known as *ubuntu*, is the foundation of African spiritual and philosophical thought.

In Buddhism, the individual self is considered to be "empty". The Vedic notion of the higher self or atman was replaced by the concept of *anatman*—literally "no self." This doesn't mean we don't exist; rather, it means that we are fundamentally relational. We give rise to one another; we depend on one another. When I try to locate my true identity in the absence of others, I find nothing. I am, in fact, the relationships I have cultivated, the air I breathe, the food I eat, the ideas I share. Imagine how different our world could be if we lived in these terms?

*   *   *

A spiritual life rooted in concepts like *ubuntu* or *anatman* isn't about individual salvation or happiness. It is about a story that connects us.

To imagine that we are part of a global community requires deep spiritual work. It has to be about worldview and story. And while the old traditions can inform us, we also need to do the work to reimagine them in ways that make sense for this unique moment.

It needn't be too complicated. Let's return to the bus. The practice is to be there, present, and to perceive and to feel our interconnectedness. We are in relationship with the other people there. We are in relationship to the birds soaring over the water. We are in relationship with the water itself. We'll soon be drinking it. Soon, our own bodies will return the water back to the lake.

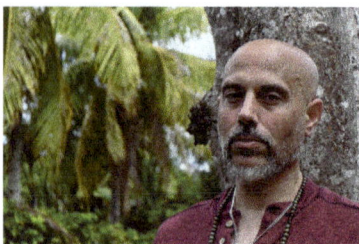

Theodore Richards (www.theodorerichards.com) is the founder of The Chicago Wisdom Project (www.chicagowisdomproject.org) and the author of seven books and numerous literary awards, including three Independent Book Awards and two Nautilus Book Awards. His most recent book is *A Letter to My Daughters: Remembering the Lost Dimension & the Texture of Life*, winner of the Independent Publisher Awards Gold Medal in memoir. He lives on the south side of Chicago with his wife and three daughters.

ESSAYS

"Resist much, obey little."
–Walt Whitman, Leaves of Grass

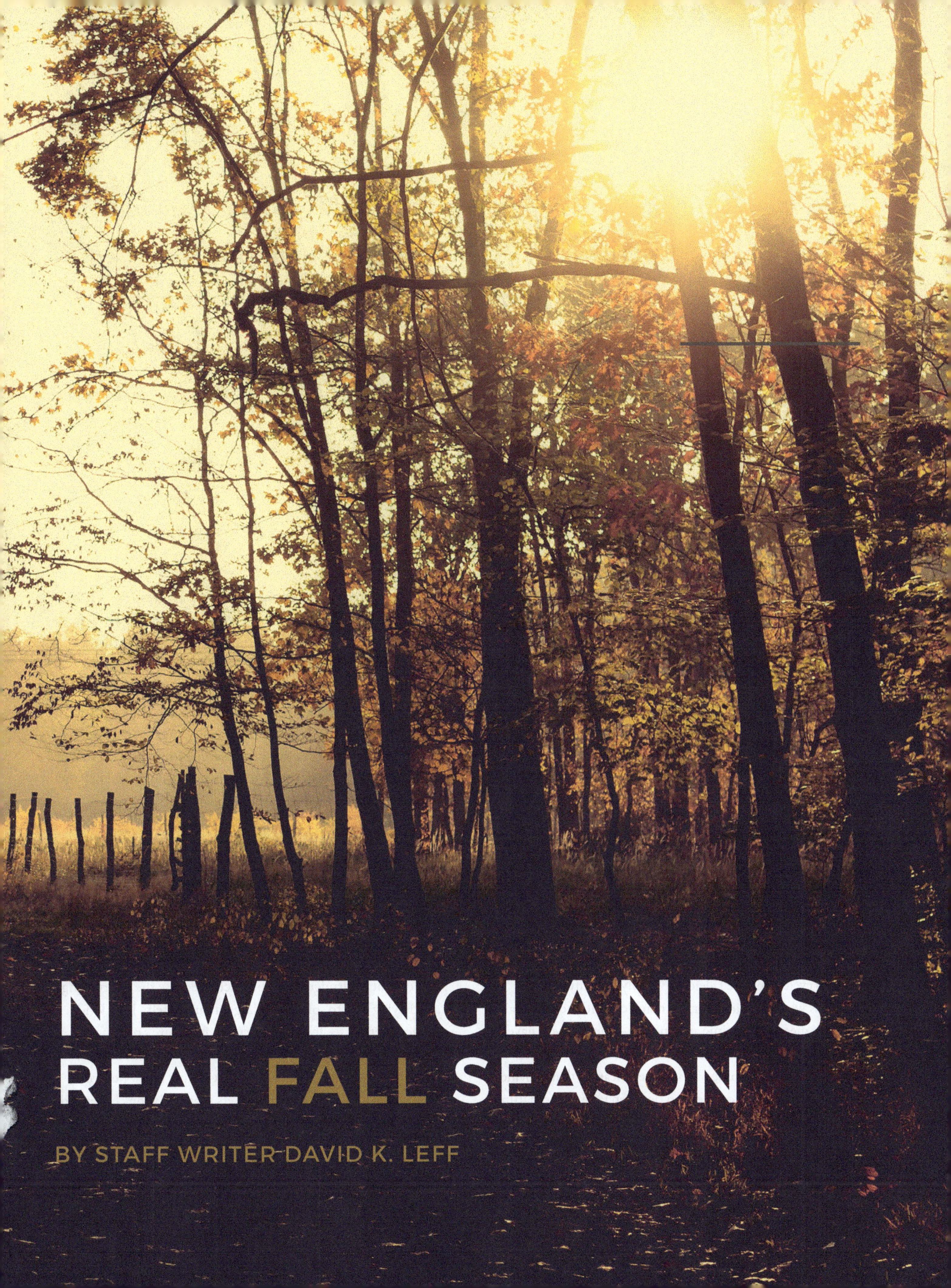

NEW ENGLAND'S REAL FALL SEASON

BY STAFF WRITER DAVID K. LEFF

"October is the month for painted leaves. Their rich glow now flashes round the world. As fruits and leaves and the day itself acquire a bright tint just before they fall so the year near its setting. October is its sunset sky; November the later twilight."

–Henry David Thoreau

It's like awakening with a hangover from a month-long party celebrated with tons of colored confetti. When leaves have dropped and leaf peeping tourists are gone, that's autumn in New England for many of us living here. Time for leaf cleanup.

We're world famous for October color. It might as well be a sunset caught for weeks like a kite in the trees. It's a regional icon essential to our identity and economy. New Englanders delight in flaming sugar maples, lemony birches, and late blushing coppery oaks. The vibrancy of the year's colors is a subject for discussion on street corners, in supermarkets, and around dinner tables. The effects of rain or drought, the previous year's snowfall, hours of sunlight, and an early or late frost are among variables providing almost as much partisan passion as politics.

Bright autumnal tints elevate the spirit, put us in touch with natural cycles, and are kaleidoscopically beautiful. But as much as we delight in color, for many of us it's not the main event as measured in time and energy—at least if you have a lawn and garden. As the season's more evocative name suggests, it's the fall of leaves and their cleanup that provides the most immediate connection between people and nature.

I find the gentle, sometimes swirling, easy float of leaves to the ground fascinating. Every year I spend hours watching them drop from the sugar maple outside my window. How soothing to see them drift down without benefit of a breeze. They are almost suspended in the air, soundless, gently rocking like tiny golden boats on water. Each one loosened from a branch is like the ticking of a seasonal clock. Then suddenly, responding to the slightest breeze, there's a whirling cascade falling with the intensity a summer cloudburst. Afterward, not a single leaf will fall for the remainder of the day. Signaling a changing year, I watch with a mixture of sadness and delight as one season is exchanged for another.

Of course, leaves falling means leaf cleanup. It can be an arduous task rivaling snow removal for the least liked necessity of yardwork. Often it involves raking, blowing, tarping, lugging, and carrying them away. And while I like watching leaves fall, to my annoyance it always seems that the wind lands the lion's share in my yard. I know my neighbors feel the same.

Yet, it's not all drudgery and backache because the effort brings a satisfying link to something larger than myself. It's a kind of sacrament, a feeling of partnership in nature's routines. Participation "in Autumn's affirmation," twentieth century writer Hal Borland called it. "In that simple task," he wrote, "I was affirming my belief in matters that are being challenged day after day. Particularly my belief in a tomorrow, a future." Routines like his annual fall composting of leaves said more to him than "loud words and the big defiances" in the public realm.

The way in which we dispose of leaves has changed a great deal over the past half century, evidence of larger factors in the world around us and rising environmental consciousness. When I was a child, those who didn't have adjacent woods to toss their leaves, raked them to the curb and burned them in slow, smoky fires. Concerns over air pollution led to bans on burning and for a period of time many leaves were dumped in landfills. With landfills reaching capacity, widescale industrial composting was implemented and leaves were forbidden in municipal trash. As Borland knew, composting not only enables us to participate in the work of the season, it produces a valuable product returned to the earth as humus, sustaining humanity with nutrients for food and fiber crops.

Live in New England long enough and leaf cleanup becomes an epic of family life, a biographical marker in the year that binds generations. Walking home from first grade in the early 1960s, I remember smoldering leaf piles along the road. They smelled vaguely sweet, slightly pungent. To me that scent remains the essence of autumn, and in memory I smell it every year though it's been many decades since I've had an actual whiff. Scamp that I was, I'd sometimes kick the burning piles and dart off before being caught. It's a wonder I didn't start any fires—at least none that I know about.

Kicking leaf piles and jumping into them was an annual ritual of my youth, well into high school. It's a pleasure I later shared with my own children, now full-fledged adults. There are few simpler and greater joys. You leap, cover yourself with leaves, breathe their earthy scent, and laugh with abandon. We wrestled in the piles and tossed leaves at each other like they were all we ever needed. The late Donald Hall, poet laureate of the United States, extoled the delights of leaf kicking in verse: "I kick at the leaves of maples, / reds of seventy different shades, yellow / like old paper; and poplar leaves, fragile and pale; / and elm leaves, flags of a doomed race."

My kids and I didn't merely kick and jump in leaves. We also collected colors and shapes, turned them into art with glue or crayons. Sometimes we ironed them between pieces of wax paper, creating our own ersatz stained glass. I did the same in grammar school.

With time's passage, autumn cleanup is marked by increasingly aching muscles as I age, and changes in leaf removal technology. Where once rakes were the primary means of gathering, now there are blowers of various kinds emitting noise that ranges from the whine of giant mosquitos, to the endless roar of motorcycles.

I still use a rake in some places, but a blower is easier on my back, if not my muff protected ears. Still, I sometimes miss the regular rhythm of the rake and its gentle scratching sound. Some people still bag their leaves for pick up, others employ elephantine vacuum trucks with giant hoses like pachyderm trunks. For years, I loaded my leaves in a pickup bed and carried them to a local farm where they were used as compost on lettuce, carrots, cucumbers and other vegetables I'd buy in season. In this small way, I tied fall labor to spring and summer meals. These days, a young landscaper gathers my leaves from the curb where I've blown and raked them.

With all the uncertainties in the world, there's something comforting in knowing that come autumn, leaves will fall and a familiar task beckon. Trees shake off the trappings of summer and so do I. There's a lot more than color to this deciduous bedtime. There's a lot more than hard work to cleaning up.

David K. Leff is an award-winning essayist, poet laureate of Canton, Connecticut, and former deputy commissioner of the Connecticut Department of Environmental Protection. By appointment of the National Park Service he served as poet-in-residence for the New England National Scenic Trail (NET) for 2016-17. View his work at www.davidkleff.com

CLIMBING THE SACRED BEAR

BY BURT BRADLEY

(ARCHIVE SPRING 2019 ISSUE. SELECTED IN MEMORY OF THE POET HIMSELF WE LOST THIS PAST YEAR.)

It is called Noavosse, "The Good Mountain," by the Cheyenne, Mato Paha, "Bear Mountain" by the Sioux, and Bear Butte by the United States Department of the Interior. A sign at the base of the mountain reads,

"Here through the centuries the Plains Indians received spiritual guidance from the creator.

Here the Cheyenne prophet, Sweet Medicine, received the four sacred arrows, the four commandments and a moral code.

Here the Sioux worshiped Wankan Tanka and paid tribute to the Spiritual Ruler."

And here, I find myself before dawn on the day after summer solstice, a man who has spent the first half of his life living at thirty-two feet above sea level with little knowledge of mountains and less knowledge of the sacred, ready to ascend.

I've come to know mountains better after first living in the Sierra Nevadas and now for the past twenty years in the Big Horn Basin in Northwest Wyoming surrounded by their rough namesakes the Absarokas, Big Horns, and Beartooth Mountains. Yet, I'm still a novice when it comes to the sacred.

Mato Paha, Bear Butte is a place of prayer and centering that is not just solitude but a meditative, vital space. It is not a place to merely relax or camp out. It is an environment in which to experience that rarest of human feelings: rapture. It is a sensual place, too, in the visionary sense of fully listening, seeing, and engaging with one's entire being. "Things" are to be experienced differently than what one experiences of life from one's front window or favorite fishing hole.

And what is it exactly that one perceives? Or, to phrase the question more accurately, not what, but how does one experience a difference, an intensification of one's senses, of one's thoughts about the nature of things, about one's life in the deepest sense?

Standing at the base of Bear Butte, I think about Black Elk, the Oglala Sioux holy man, who over a century earlier on a mountain top fifty miles to the south had his great vision of the world:

"And while I stood there I saw more than I can tell, and I understood more than I saw; for I was seeing in a sacred manner the shapes of all things in the spirit, and the shape of all shapes as they must live together like one being."

Visions are an inquiry into the larger questions, beliefs, and ideas in life regarding one's way of being in the world, one's direction, one's knowledge, one's relationship to others and to the whole overall. Not that the little, everyday life is ignored but it is to be seen through a wider lens, *in a sacred manner.*

You can photograph the mountain from the parking lot, or you can camp out at Bear Butte Lake two miles away. But to experience the sacredness of the place you need to climb. I decide to walk up just before sunrise. It is a pristine summer morning and my mood has already been enhanced by the lingering atmosphere of religious ceremonies conducted the previous four days as part of a summer solstice celebration.

I was allowed to stay in the empty camp at the base of the mountain. I pitched my tent among abandoned sweat lodges and communal fire pits with various "altars" of stones, feathers, and prayer cloths—not to mention the campsite of an old Lakota man, who sang until midnight accompanied by a drum.

I spent the night by a fire, listening to him talking to some friends, low, good friend talk, barely audible, no louder than the occasional bird whistle, the loon clarinet in the distance, the murmuring creek, the slight breeze whispering through the trees.

So, the hike itself is charged before I take my first step. I am a mixture of eagerness and slight apprehension. Should I? Am I worthy? Can I do this right? I carry with me a gift of prayer tobacco from my friend Jenny who said it is for homage, adding with a smile, "And a little insurance." For or against what, I wasn't sure. The sun slowly appears, first as a mere lighting of the far sky, and then on the furthest plains, the last long shadow of night shrinking its way toward me at the foot of the mountain.

I begin to walk up the mountain, keeping the same pace as the retreating shadow, eventually letting it overtake me, the gray air becoming light, revealing the rocky incline, talus cracking under my feet. I am met with the sweet scent of purple and yellow flowers and especially the white capped aroma (slightly sour at first then sweet) of wild yarrow. Brightly colored prayer cloths flap from buffalo berry bushes and ponderosa pine. Soon it is mountain sparrows and robins and luminous yellow gold finches come to greet me. And here, a butterfly planted on a bush, wings opening and closing in a slow, halting, silent applause.

It is a walk that also becomes a heaviness in my thighs, a shortness in my breathing, until I must pause, a respite, my hand timidly on the burnt bark of a dead pine (remnant from the devastating fire of 1996).

Half way up the southern slope, with still another 700 feet of hiking around to the east and up to the peak, I look back down. There spreads the Great Plains in a series of sloping undulations of new summer green, some places clotted with stands of cottonwood trees, the rest grass— presently green. But come the first full week of rainless, wind- scoured sunlight, it will redden for a day or two then gradually fade to a brownless brown, its natural, "Great Plains" coloring. For now: green space, seemingly endless, that is somewhat shocking from this first view a thousand feet up and away from the flat stretch of highway.

A flicker of color nearby—a bird or flower or prayer cloth alive in the wind, a spirit reminding me of where I am, of what this mountain has been all about, and personally, what the task is before me.

Onward and upward, I march, not Boy Scout style or as a strolling tourist with the proverbial camera banging my chest. The sign at the trail head suggested, "Whisper when talking to others." I take this to mean a deeper task for one alone. For me, this means trying to hush my "monkey mind" as the Buddhists call it, the incessant chatter in my head of all that life I left back down the hill. Like a crazed short-wave radio operator late at night who can't just listen to one signal for more than thirty seconds, my mind still "broadcasts" snippets of conversations, some overheard, some still engaged in. They range from the previous night to the day before that, some a month old, some ten years earlier— an old argument, a miscommunication ("What I meant to say..."), a lingering critical judgment ("If I were her, I'd...") —until it all runs together to become, finally, nothing but static.

Immediately, almost angrily, I remind myself to pay attention.

Pay attention. Pay as in giving something. A tithe, a donation, an offering of respect, of consciousness, of mindfulness. Attention as in listening. To the chirps, the buzzes, the crunching under my shoes, and the pockets of silence in between, reminding me where I am, not who. And what I am doing at this very moment, not before or later. Pay attention to the rock I've just stumbled over. To the next step. And the next. To the sharp light splashed on the bearberry bushes. To the sudden sweet scent of some mountain flower or the odd oil-burnt smell of creosote on the logs lining the path. Shhhhhh. Walk, breathe, sense.

I resume, quieter somewhat, slower. In no hurry. The pace of my ascent now coinciding with the rising sun. I look at the fiery orb, a hand rubbed, polished apple— Golden Delicious—hanging from a branch of sky just

above the horizon. I feel its first heat and strip off my lined, flannel shirt. Immediately, I grow thinner, lighter, more flexible, but also more vulnerable as I ascend. I try to fight off the nagging thought of unworthiness, of being spiritually "incorrect." I stop, turn, and see that the plains are now brilliantly lit, and incredibly, have grown larger, greener.

I stand next to a stone outcropping with yellowish lichen marbling its north face. I pull out the Kinnick Kinnick, traditional ceremonial tobacco of bearberry, red willow, osha root, mullen, and yerba santa—friend Jenny's gift. I hold a pinch of it out before me and realize I'm at a loss for words. I feel intimidated by the responsibility of the act. I wish to do this right. Me, some middle-aged, would-be apprentice without a master.

I begin by thanking the mountain directly for allowing me to be here. I offer a blessing which I hope doesn't sound too much to me like my father's terse grace at Thanksgiving, Easter, and Christmas (terse because the act reminded him of his Southern Baptist heritage which

he had abandoned long ago). I toss the tobacco out like a farmer scattering feed, and surprisingly feel more valid, though still unsteady. I move on.

Finally nearing the peak, I stop again, mainly to resist my European heritage of "having to get to the top." Why? What is the point? "Because it is there," declared the first white man (with Sherpa guides) to scale Mt. Everest, Sir Edmund Hillary. From what little I know about him, he was a man who seemed to have had a reverence for mountains.

I try to think of his statement from a Zen Buddhist's perspective. "Because it is there" does not connote climbing simply for fun or fame or ego gratification. If declared with a spiritual meaning, then the statement cannot be equated with an insidious notion of, "I conquered the mountain," or "I claim this mountain..." Rather, "Because it is there" is a wonderful Zen statement, filled with meaningfulness, yet completely understated, to the point of irony, even absurdity. "The sword that kills the man is the sword that saves the man."

"Because it is there" beckons to me. It is a spiritual challenge for me to experience this mountain more fully than I have. To put it another way, "Because it is there," I must. Or, "Because it is there," and I am not. It is a challenge for me to grasp what it means to "get to the top."

With such thoughts, I climb the last fifty feet to the peak. My first decision is to avoid the large wooden, designated lookout platform. Not without some trepidation, I follow a barely discernible footpath that traverses the ridge to the south. There's one of those Park Service trail signs with a figure with a walking stick and back pack hiking inside a red circle with a red line through it. One thing I am clear about: I am not hiking. I step out on the path already lined with prayer cloths and offerings with as pure an intention as possible: I'm here to offer a blessing, to give thanks, to sprinkle some ceremonial tobacco, and to practice zazen, sitting meditation, (my only "formal" praying).

And sitting among the prayer cloths, the small stone "altars" and cairns with various offerings adorning them, I am most mindful of the space I inhabit, the heady wind, the girth of mountain beneath me, the brassy light, and an odd species of flies. They are as large as small bees, but they don't zoom all about like the common house fly.

Instead, they hold still in mid-air, much like a dragonfly, buzzing as they do, seeming to watch me. After awhile, a couple "bump" me here and there, on an elbow, a forearm, the top of my head—Am I spirit or flesh? Am I being respectful? These are the guardians I think—maybe even the spirits of the ancestors themselves. I try to stay centered as long as possible...longer. This means losing my "I." Instead, be here and nothing else, but present in the sharp rocks, the ponderosa pine riffling with color, the prayer cloths alive in the stiff breeze that remind me I will not fool anyone here, especially myself.

This isn't a game. This isn't "cool," or a "Wait until I tell somebody" opportunity. This is, for me, my practice, my best effort at faith, which Katagiri Roshi says is neither something given by somebody, nor is it something coming from you. Rather, "Faith means tranquility, and complete tranquility is the source of our nature and our existence."

I gradually move out of silent, sitting meditation to consciously ask for blessings—for my daughters, my son, my wife, all my loved ones, friends, family, past and present and future—as heartfelt and mindfully as possible. My heart is moved to ask for a blessing for "all sentient beings," as the Buddhist vow puts it. I take vows and offer prayers for the earth itself. I ask for nothing in return, except for assistance to honor life in all of its manifestations, to continually cherish life with clarity, conviction, and courage.

I manage to meditate about twenty minutes I guess, maybe thirty. I'm not that strong spiritually yet. It takes great strength to worship—to surrender to that which one barely comprehends, to give up one's intellect, one's reason, to "think," instead, with the heart, to open oneself up to intuition, to intimation, to a felt sense of the world, to the energy of the world, to the spirit of the world. This is the kind of spiritual strength one finds in the figures of Moses, Jesus, Buddha, Mohammed, Crazy Horse, Black Elk and, our own times, in a Gandhi, a Martin Luther King Jr., a Mother Theresa. Giant shoes to fill, I know, but footsteps, nonetheless, to follow.

Still, though I have meditated only thirty minutes, the act feels thorough, focused. As my ego dissolves, I experience this mountain as a site of the earth's power, a spiritual capitol of the world.

Later, on the South Dakota State Park observation platform, I find I am unable to write poetry. I can't "stop" experiencing the dynamics of the place—though writing, poetry, is often a way of connecting for me, of becoming an integral part of the process of being in a place, or of consciously participating in an event, never with the "objectivity" of a reporter or scientist, but subjectively, sympathetically, intimately as a poet. At the moment, however, this is just not to be.

But I do have another way of praying. Laying down my pencil and notebook, I began to dance Tai chi. I practice a version called "Embrace Tiger, Return to Mountain" that incorporates the five elements (fire, water, wood, metal, earth) into the dance. Dancing Tai chi brings me physically into accord with the movements of wind, trees, prayer cloths, flies, sun, and space—the feeling of being on top of a mountain, of moving in a slow circle following the sun, east to west. Afterwards, I am inspired to write.

Atop this great wave of earth, I dance,

the ground below humming roots.

These feet rise and fall slowly

to a song of breathing, falling

and rising within this wooded space:

this body becoming tree, pine fleshed,

arms branching into the blue air,

where these hands grow wings

and circle in the fledgling light.

A half hour later, the sun, a young ponderosa pine higher, I see far down the mountain. Ranger vehicles already in the parking lots, and a mile away the first visitor at the gate, and a half mile further back turning off the main highway another visitor's car. I estimate they will be up here within an hour. My time, alone, with the spirit of the place is ending. And yet I linger not ten feet from the steps of the platform on the way back down. There's one more task I need to perform.

What is it? I sit, listening to the wind sighing through the blackened bones of the pines. Later, Bear Butte State Park Ranger Chuck Rambow tells me the Native Americans

say the Great Spirit saved the mountain from being completely burnt. But it was a terrific fire, devastating. Approximately, ninety percent of the trees on Bear Butte were either consumed by the fire or scorched to a point where recovery is unlikely. The Lakotas I spoke with the night before insinuated it was "non-native people" who started it—accidentally.

But it seemed, to me, something was a bit askew with their tale and with all "accidents." The emphasis shouldn't be on who is to blame; it doesn't have anything to do with blame. Even the Lakota seemed uncomfortable with their own explanation. I heard an uncertainty in their voices as they told me about the "campfire that wasn't extinguished properly." They spoke with more conviction when they mentioned "a big wind," and that there had been a drought.

Finally, everyone agrees in hindsight—Cheyenne, Lakota, and Ranger Rambow. It has been a purification wrought by the Creator. Everything is better today, despite the loss of ponderosa pine and the frequent mud slides; there is much new grass, even an abundance of the precious "June" grass used in Sundance ceremonies.

The day before, I met a blithe, young woman, who worked in the information booth at the Bear Butte trail head. She was chatty, spilling over with youth's sense of its own vitality. She informed me the journey up the mountain was an "easy hike" of about an hour and a half, and a half hour down. "You could be done in no time."

Recalling her statement, I laugh quietly and am tempted to say to the sky, "Out of the mouth of babes." But, I don't. As I begin my descent, however, I assume a "no-time" attitude and begin walking mindfully one step at a time. In step with my breathing. I center my concentration in my hara, my lower abdomen below my navel. Centered and centerless, this is kinhin, slow walking meditation one practices between periods of formal sitting meditation in the zendo.

I walk, neither stuck in my own thoughts, nor attached to the phenomenal world about me. If anything, my focus is somewhere between both. For when I am feeling particularly right, out there and inside are indistinguishable. During such clear moments, a pebble glinting in the sunlit path at my feet, glistens inside me. Again, to use Zen phrasing, I walk mindfully.

Not I am walking down the mountain, but I am the mountain's walking consciousness. I am its slope, its talus, its altitude, its gravity in my calves and thighs, its eyes— seeing a mountain sparrow nearly invisible, mottled brown as the tree limb on which it perches. I am the mountain rose, the wild yarrow that rings the top in clusters of white cupped flowers. I am the mountain's ears, its listening to the wind, to the birds, to a jet 35,000 feet overhead, and to a single car winding its way toward the visitor's center a mile and half below. I am also the mountain's fingers and feet. As well as the mountain's mood of serenity and expansiveness, its warming beneath the rising sun, its lingering coolness in the shade on its unlit north side. The Zen Master, Dogen uses the term "whole faith-like body," which means your whole body and mind are exactly faith. It is with this kind of "whole faith-like body," that I descend the mountain.

I notice a butterfly moving alongside of me, moving as I move. It has black wings with splotches of white. It stays with me for twenty, thirty yards. I can't help but think of it as escorting me on my way, a guide, a guardian, a fellow sentient being. And then just as it stops, landing on a white flower on the up slope, another butterfly appears, tangerine colored with black spots, and immediately begins to escort me for the next twenty or thirty yards. It is one of the most simple, silent, and subtle of events, and yet beaming with awe and gratitude for the attention

I halt, again perhaps halfway, my hand against calcite rock. There a fly an inch from my index finger. I move ever so slightly toward it and it moves minutely toward me. It walks onto my fingernail. I make no motion to brush it off. In fact, I carefully move my hand back to its kinhin position over the other folded across my lower belly and continue walking meditation.

Nothing misses my attention and, yet my attention holds onto nothing. Each flat stone step every twenty-five feet or so, strategically placed where the path switchbacks, traversing its way back and forth down the hill. Each twig, each scattered leaf, the peppering of shade and light across the rock-strewn path.

For the Lakota, this mountain (particularly the southern slope) represents the bear of the Devil's Tower myth, who after futilely attempting to reach the young princesses (or warriors depending on who tells the tale), gave up and wandered the fifty miles to this part of South Dakota, where it lay down to become Bear Butte. But I'm still on the eastern slope, which is the "Cheyenne side" of the mountain that they see as a great sacred lodge where their folk hero, Sweet Medicine, received the Four Sacred Arrows, the medicine laws of the tribe.

In the past, these myths seemed historically and culturally so far away from me. Yet, here I expect at any moment during my descent to meet one of the Old Ones, maybe

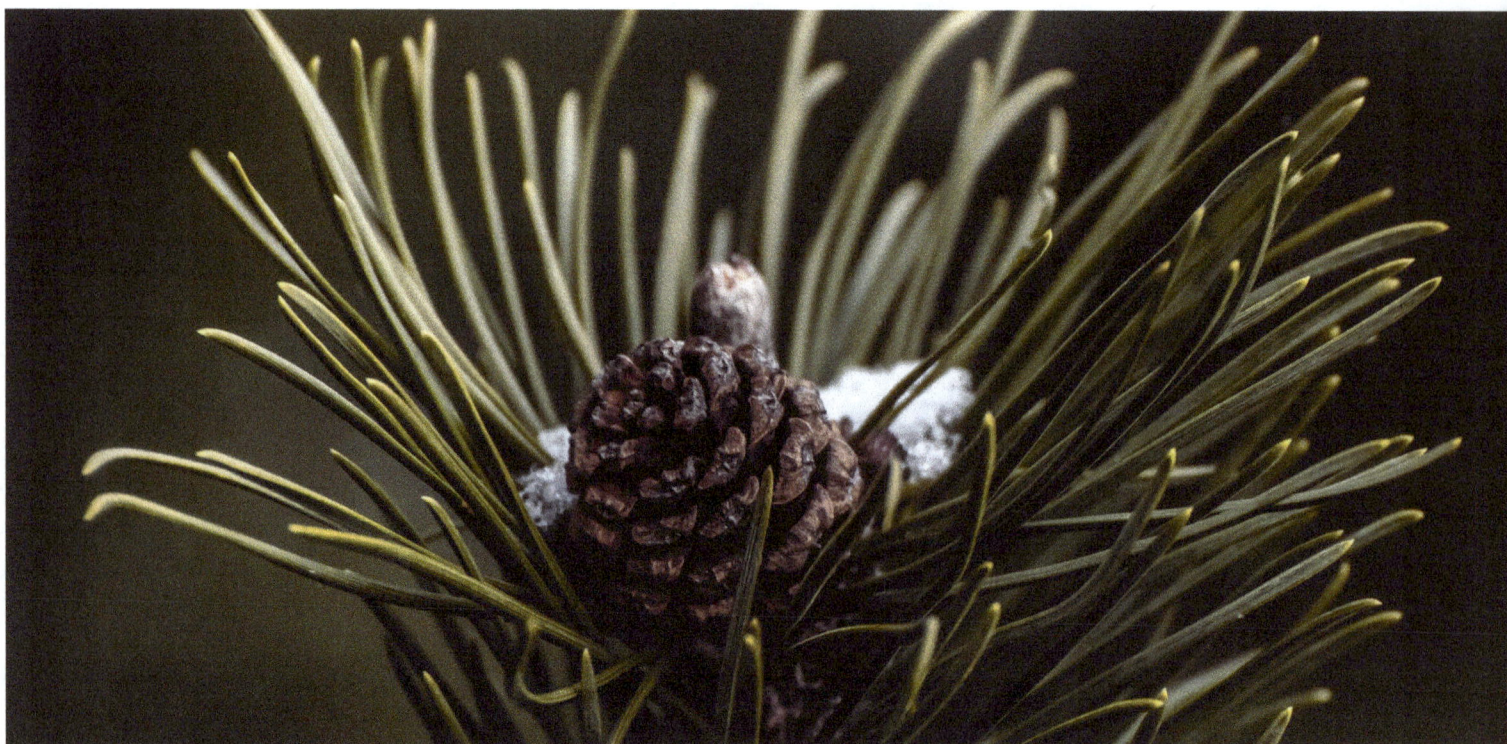

Sweet Medicine himself. I wonder what sort of sacred bundle I might receive? Is there something I can take back to America at the beginning of the Twenty First Century?

I descend, my body and mind attuned to the details of the place. I glance down at the fly still sitting on my hand, silent, motionless. It waits too. My spirit guide? This insignificant, even reprehensible creature, what truth could it carry? I know the common attitude. But, I still resist swatting at it and choose instead to walk with it as my guide. In and out of the dappled light and shadow, I inhale the subtle and rich scent of pine and flowers I cannot name.

And the colors! Here and there in certain patches of bright light, a burst of magenta and fuchsia and deep purple, splashes of creamy yellow and sky blue. I can't imagine what the fly sees with its magnified sense of seeing, but to me, the colors are so vivid as to be fully meaningful as simply color for its own sake.

As if on cue upon reaching a certain boundary, the fly tickles my hand as it moves for the first time, perhaps not more than a millimeter, before flying off. Thirty seconds later, I encounter the first humans of the day, a young couple, walking fast, but quietly. We pass without eye contact, wordlessly. The mountain gives us permission to do this without guilt or feelings of uneasiness.

Then not long, three men, middle-aged, loud talking, kicking rocks, stumbling, laughing. "How's it going?" the first booms. Cameras around their necks, sweating already, no doubt in a hurry to get to the top, take their pictures, remark about the view, then scramble down to where next? Devil's Tower to the west? Mt. Rushmore to the south? A casino in Deadwood?

The last fellow erupts, huffing to me, "Bet it's easier going down!"

I steel myself, trying to not pass judgment (though I already have). They will receive what they bring in their hearts. The mountain is ancient, imperturbable, mysterious. Spiritual responses—whether rewards or repercussions—are unfathomable. Those who believe, who have faith, and who act accordingly, are astute and will be the first to recognize the movement of spirit. Life begins with suffering, says the Buddha, and yet he is often depicted smiling. He's not amused by distress, but at peace because he understood the cause (ignorance) and the cure (knowledge) and the result (enlightenment).

Here, back in my living room, I'm smiling, too. Not because I know what the Buddha knows, but because six months have passed since that predawn hike and I have not left Bear Butte. Or, rather, Bear Butte has not left me. I don't mean, however, just in the sense of memory, of mentally recalling that time on the sacred mountain. Rather, practicing sitting meditation looking out the window, I am again experiencing a feeling of centeredness. The Buddhists declare, "Everything is Mind," or as Dogen puts it, "The entire universe is the human body." My feeling of centeredness when climbing Bear Butte and my feeling of centeredness looking out my window are the same feeling, the same insight, the same center of this entire universe. As Black Elk explained his vision atop Mt. Harney: "I saw myself on the central mountain of the world, the highest place...But, the central mountain is everywhere." Everywhere being Mt. Harney, Bear Butte, and Heart Mountain four miles from this living room floor here where I am sitting gazing out the window as winter begins to solidify around my house *in a sacred manner.*

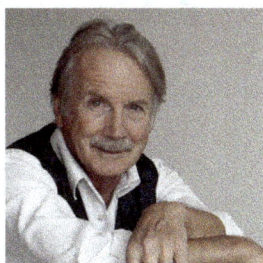

Burt Bradley lived on a bluff in Northwest Wyoming seventy miles from Yellowstone National Park. For over thirty years, with his wife Janet, a photographer, he has delved into the wild serenity of the greater Yellowstone ecosystem. His writing has appeared in *Ring of Fire: Writers of the Yellowstone Region, Michigan Quarterly Review, Best of Writers at Work,* among others. He was a professor emeritus at Northwest College in Powell, Wyoming, where he taught Writing in the Wild classes in Yellowstone and the Southwest Desert. This first poetry collection, *After Following,* won the Homebound Publications Poetry Prize and is now available. This posthumous collection, *Letters to Michelangelo from Wyoming,* is now available wherever books are sold.

FROM DISTRESS TO STRENGTH

BY STAFF WRITER IRIS GRAVILLE

Very early in Heidi Barr's book, *What Comes Next: Between Beauty and Destruction* (Homebound Publications, 2019) I felt a shiver of empathy as I read about a phone call she received. "Hello, Heidi," her supervisor said one morning. "We regret to inform you that as of December 2nd, your position is being eliminated." What follows that early scene is the story of how Heidi dived head first into a season of discernment, pondering productivity and worth, privilege and what ifs, and success and meaning.

Heidi's story brought back memories of my own job loss years ago.

After nearly twenty years as a nurse, most of them in public health, I had wanted to try my hand at management. When the communicable disease supervisor position at the county health department where I worked opened, I applied and was promoted. While I'd felt competent as a staff nurse in the maternal-child health division there, I was once again a novice. I scrambled to learn about childhood and travel immunizations, communicable disease outbreaks, and staff supervision. Throughout eighteen months of challenges with an E. coli outbreak, a potential measles outbreak, and conflicts with administrators, I couldn't quiet my doubts about my abilities.

Those qualms flooded me when the county council mandated a cut in middle management, and my position was combined with another supervisor role. As the most recently hired, I was bumped out of my post. Fortunately, my union contract required I be offered another position, and there was a communicable disease staff nurse opening. While I still had a job and was grateful for it, it wasn't one I would have chosen.

I'd never "lost" a job. Even though my director assured me it wasn't because of my ability, I couldn't shake the belief I was downgraded because I'd failed as a supervisor. And failure? That was unfamiliar territory, too.

Beginning in my early twenties, I assumed I'd work as a nurse all my life, in fact, that I was a nurse to my very core. When peers talked about living for their days off when they could do what they really loved, I felt deep gratitude I'd been led to a career that was so much more than a job to me. I treasured the ways it sated my curiosity about anatomy, physiology, and pathophysiology at the same time it offered an outlet for my compassion for others. My work and my desire to serve had coalesced.

Heidi's recognition that "...beauty is best uncovered in the rubble of destruction" can be a balm in such unsettled times— whether they involve a pink slip or some other challenge.

The demotion, however, coupled with dissatisfaction in my new staff nurse position, opened me to consider other possibilities. Perhaps I was being called to different work and service. To be honest, though, it wasn't so much opening a door as being pushed through it.

At the height of feeling lost about my purpose, my family vacationed in Stehekin, a tiny, remote village in Washington's North Cascades. Its name, a Coast Salish word, means "the way through."

We'd visited Stehekin annually for ten years and always spent some of that time fantasizing about living there. We also always talked ourselves out of the idea by the end of our stay. That year of my job loss, though, in Stehekin's solitude and silence, the draw to a different way of life pulled and wouldn't let go.

After months of discernment, my husband, our two kids, and I reached clarity to move to Stehekin. I chronicle that decision and what followed in my memoir *Hiking Naked: A Quaker Woman's Search for Balance* (Homebound Publications, 2018). Like Heidi, I drew on the wisdom of writers, poets, trusted friends, and the natural world to yield, rather than fight, to let life's purpose in.

Spoiler alert for *What Comes Next*: Heidi found new strength after receiving a pink slip. She did it in her own way, in a place that spoke to her. As she writes, "There is beauty, and there is destruction, and they are existing side by side. This is not new—it's been happening since the dawn of time. It will keep happening for the rest of my human lifetime. So, my plan

is to take the beauty that I find wherever I am, whatever my employment status, whatever life decides to dish out next, and use it to fuel myself with active hope."

Spoiler alert for *Hiking Naked*: I don't live in Stehekin anymore. But it lives in me in the memories of black bears playing in the yard, forest fires, record-breaking floods, day hikes and cross-country skiing in the backcountry, star-filled skies, and the kind of quiet you only find far from heavily-trafficked roadways.

What lives on the most is what was not in Stehekin —the drive to always move faster and the unrelenting press to consume. It was the absences—of television, phones, shopping malls, limitless options—that encouraged and sometimes forced me to look inward.

Far from feeling deprived in Stehekin, I found over and over again the riches of attending to what's truly important. These days, I continue to seek the way through as I learned to do in that earlier period of vulnerability. Heidi's recognition that "... beauty is best uncovered in the rubble of destruction" can be a balm in such unsettled times—whether they involve a pink slip or some other challenge.

Now, nearly two years into the COVID-19 pandemic, I wonder about others questioning what's most essential. Many have lost not only jobs, but also friends, family, and a sense of certainty about the future. I hope Heidi's story, and mine, might ease some of the distress and inspire strength and hope for the days of discernment ahead.

Iris Graville is the author of three nonfiction books: *Hands at Work, BOUNTY*, and a memoir, *Hiking Naked.* She lives on Lopez Island, WA where she publishes SHARK REEF Literary Magazine, writes essays and blogs, and teaches. Sometimes you'll find her on the interisland ferry, working on a new essay collection about the Salish Sea, climate change, and Washington State Ferries. irisgraville.com.

THE MINDFUL KITCHEN

LIFE UNFOLDING & BLACK BEAN TACO SALAD

THE MINDFUL KITCHEN BY HEIDI BARR

Raise your hand if you have ever been impatient when it comes to seeing results.

Everyone raises their hands, including me.

Humans seem wired to strive, to grow, to seek improvement. (Even if we're not actually wired for this, that's what our culture teaches us to do. Unpacking that is a column for another day...) When it comes to growth, or perhaps we can say "positive evolution toward wellbeing", so often the desire is to just get there already. Make the desired changes and be done with it. Yet every human is a unique, continually unfolding, work of art—YOU are a continually unfolding work of art—a life continually coming more fully into itself. That positive evolution of maintaining optimal wellbeing is a lifelong project. It can feel like the road is entirely uphill and bumpy, but taking one step after another (no matter how small) keeps you moving toward the good stuff.

You are living a life in progress, and life unfolds one step at a time.

Note: Cultivating patience and the capacity for sitting with negative emotions makes this more bearable.

Unsolicited advice isn't always the most helpful when it comes to creating positive change in your life, but on occasion, having some ideas on how to keep on keepin' on can be useful.

Award winning author of several books, Heidi Barr is committed to cultivating ways of being that are life-giving and sustainable for people, communities and the planet. She works as a wellness coach, holds a Master's degree in Faith and Health Ministries and occasionally partners with organic farms and yoga teachers to offer retreat experiences. At home in Minnesota, she lives with her husband and daughter where they tend a large vegetable garden, explore nature and do their best to live simply. Visit her at www.heidibarr.com

1. PRACTICE GRATITUDE:

You've heard this before, many times. The thing is, it works. Think of something small you're grateful for right now, and then extend gratitude to yourself for taking the time to reflect. Repeat frequently.

2. KEEP MOVING:

Do at least one movement every day that feels good. This can be any activity that gets you up and going, whatever 'up and going' looks like for your life situation and ability level. No formal workout routines required.

3. EAT PLANTS:

This may seem obvious, but eating a diet rich in fruits and vegetables is essential, so it's worth repeating, even if I'm preaching to the choir. As Michael Pollan said, "Eat food. Not too much. Mostly plants." Good advice, that. Pick one new plant to try this week.

4. STAND (OR SIT) MINDFULLY:

Pay attention to your posture. Roll your shoulders back and down. Take a few deep breaths and notice how your body connects to whatever's supporting it right now. Remember you're a living, breathing, human animal.

5. LOVE THE WORLD.

This one's not so simple, right? There's a lot not to love about the world. Yet, there's work to be done, and acting from love —of self, of neighbor, of stranger— allows love to take on a body and take another step toward a more beautiful world.

Practice steps one through five and see how things unfold.

When it comes to eating more plants......

BLACK BEAN TACO SALAD

Serves two as a main dish

INGREDIENTS

- 1 can of black beans (or any bean of your choice)
- 3-4 cups of greens (chopped lettuce, kale, or chard)
- 1 red or yellow bell pepper, diced
- 1 tomato, diced (or use cherry tomatoes, halved)
- 1 small zucchini, diced
- 1 avocado, sliced
- ½ cup cheddar cheese
- Cilantro, chopped

DRESSING

- ¼ cup sour cream
- ¼ cup olive oil
- 2 TB white wine vinegar
- Juice of one whole lime
- Garlic salt (to taste)

DIRECTIONS

Drain and rinse black beans and place in a small saucepan. Add a few tablespoons of taco seasoning or cumin and chili powder, along with a few tablespoons of water. Heat to desired temperature.

Place lettuce in two bowls, and add other ingredients as desired.

Shake the salad ingredients in a small lidded jar and drizzle on assembled salad.

POETRY

"Poetry is the shadow cast by our streetlight imaginations."
–Lawrence Ferlinghetti

ANDREW JARVIS

WILDERNESS RENTAL

The cabin has a sunset view,
cabana chairs, and tree hammocks
for lounging with the animals.

Tiki torches carefully placed
beside the hot tub, grill, and bar
mark luau nights in wilderness.

With furnished guest rooms, bathrooms,
and kitchen, it is a rugged
experience with bald eagles.

Guests will see reindeer, bears, falcons,
huskies, orcas, salmon, and whales
from a private beach and fire pit.

Ice is available, but guests
mostly prefer fresh glacier
water for frozen daiquiris.

Electricity and water
are included, along with free
fish gummies for the little ones.

Free nights, if booked in advance,
along with wild welcome gifts,
to live in nature for sale.

LOAM

Our sand, silt, and clay composite
is ready for plowing in rows

of organic wheat, where we stretch
our toes in soil, for its soothing

warmth in a field of memories,
where we planted before winter

in our permanent sow of wealth,
cultivated, ready to grow

into eternal feed, for life,
where mechanical grain grinders

mill away all natural meals
for market, for the bottom line;

but we refuse to mechanize
into the overprocessed

today, instead walking within
our solid roots, our family core

of crowns, tillers, leaves, our living,
devoured, eaten, earthen.

Andrew Jarvis is the author of *Sound Points, Ascent, The Strait,* and *Landslide.* He was a Finalist for the 2014 Homebound Publications Poetry Prize, and he has received several honors from *Foreword Reviews'* INDIE Book of the Year Awards. He also received Silver Medals in Poetry from the Nautilus Book Awards and CIPA EVVY Book Awards. Andrew holds an M.A. in Writing from Johns Hopkins University.

RICK BENJAMIN

CANDLE-POD ACACIA

Just because someone wants
to devour you doesn't mean
you have to let them. Acacia
senses presence of giraffes
& will send out a certain
sourness to its leaf-tips &

pods to stop them feeding
on their top-most branches.
Better, they can send down-
wind signals to rest
of their kind in any stand,
cough up what's bitter

up-bones skyward. Spirit
resists being eaten when
someone else's hunger
says danger's nearby. Best
to throw off scents from
your darkest places, the ones

that put off even you. Maybe
later you'll be ready for that
new becoming, right when
it takes you in: long-

necked trees
camouflaged

in spots, heads
bowed toward

root of
it all.

THE DAY OUT OF TIME

First, a dog named Sirius, rises
with the sun, stretches, shines
in a star worth thirteen moons.

Call it a day of realignment to
the non-human, free, fully off-
calendar, a liminal space after

any gestation, the brief pause
that might contain a new life
beyond this one, all the laws

of our life experience held
in the feminine, 260 days,
give or take, until another

birth. But don't get ahead
of yourself. First, the dog
who is also a star rises on

a twenty-fifth day of the
seventh month, yawns
or longs out a fourth

dimension, eternal
time, where any-
might happen

& then does.

Rick Benjamin lives on Chumash land in Goleta, California, and tries to remind himself of that fact that each day as he walks ancient trails near his house. Currently teaching a range of courses at the University of California Santa Barbara, ranging from poetry and community, the wild literature of ecology, and the literatures of both social and juvenile justice. He served as the Poet Laureate of Rhode Island from 2012 – 2016.

SCOTT EDWARD ANDERSON

UNDER THE LINDEN'S SPELL

Honey and lemon-peel scent
of the linden tree's pale-yellow flowers
in drooping cymes, late June in the air—
early summer of Brooklyn,
early summer of our love.

We breathed in air rich with its flower's
scent, mingled with our own of lovers spent,
our trunks entwined like Baucis and Philemon—
my oak to your basswood—abundance overflowing,
as we drank from Mercury's Pitcher.

Scott Edward Anderson is the author of Dwelling: an ecopoem, Fallow Field, and Walks in Nature's Empire. He has been a Concordia Fellow at the Millay Colony for the Arts and received the Nebraska Review Award. His poetry has appeared in *The American Poetry Review, Alaska Quarterly Review, Cimarron Review, The Cortland Review, The Wayfarer,* and two anthologies. His essays and reviews have appeared in *basalt, The Bloomsbury Review, Cleaver, the Philadelphia Inquirer,* and elsewhere. For many years, he has worked in conservation, social enterprise, and clean energy consulting with such organizations as The Nature Conservancy, Ashoka, VerdeStrategy, and EY. He lives in Brooklyn, NY, with his wife, Samantha, and their blended family.

THE PRE-DAWN SONG OF THE PEARLY-EYED THRASHER

(Margarops fuscatus)

What are you searching for, morning visitor?
A scrap of fruit or nut, an avocado or an orange
to peck into like the egg of some competitor—

Or perhaps you are looking,
with your pearlescent eye,
for some kind of friendship—

Friendship with a kindred spirit,
one who sees, like you do, there are dangers
out there, dangers and uncertainty.

Someone who knows, as you do, survival
depends upon pursuing what you want
without regrets, but with grace and humility.

That, along with a gift for mimicry
and choices based upon trust relationships,
will help you get ahead in this world, my friend.

Or do you seek simply another being who understands
the true meaning of your pre-dawn song's "eeuu"
—and doesn't mind its melodious monotony:

I am, I am, I am.

GWENDOLYN MORGAN

—

SHE (WHO) LISTENS TO BOTANICALS

She walks through a recent burn, wildfire
this year fire travelled fifty miles an hour

flames leaped over stretches, patches left unburned
torched wild grasses, wild flowers

firestorms left remnants of gray powder
ashes, organic material vaporized

Douglas Fir may mitigate climate change
like her, better without fire.

She studies brush lettering, line drawing
her botanicals in shapes of cuneiform

wedges, wishes, living wills
light yellow green, sap green inscriptions

lichens, mosses, ferns smoldering
with stories, edible thistle

herbaceous biennial, balsam root
strong starches, impressions

She listens to their ancestors
cellular manuscripts of her descendants.

SHE (WHO) REMEMBERS AUTUMN

i's dotted with Ibis and Iceland Gull
t's crossed with Treecreeper and Tawny Owl
she says to notice this turning of the planet
the wheel of the year, Mabon to Samhain
thickening rain clouds like blackberry pie filling
nimbostratus rain clouds, cumulonimbus
clumps of thunder heads on the hills above
streaks of lightning, fires in the forest
nothing is black and white, she says
open the anthology of bird tracks
study strata, bones, sugar content
eight planets in retrograde
autumnal migration
immigrants, refugees in unsafe shelters
food shortages, food solidarity
her shoulders ache from bending
over her work in the world
the scapula, bones where the wings used to be
her memories briefly sketched in graphite and fatigue
appear as distance, absence, sorrow, fire
she gathers root vegetables, leaves of weeds
excerpts and line drawings of contour feathers, birds
she says be open to receive
messages from the universe.

Gwendolyn Morgan earned an M.F.A. in Creative Writing from Goddard College, and an M.Div. from San Francisco Theological Seminary and the Graduate Theological Union. She was the Clark County Poet Laureate 2018-2020 in Washington State.

ABIGAIL PROUT

MOTHER TREE

Calm and weary tree lean down
cover me in fragrant gold
to melt like chocolate rain in bark
like sheep into the fold

Of sinner's heart and wooden flesh
I warmly tangle in it
I marry bones and blood to dirt
and am complete this minute

There is a union sitting here
Of roots and toes and soil
Nature's fiber goulash stirred
And slowly comes to boil

Of lover's heart and wooden flesh
I sweetly tangle in it
I marry heart and mind to Earth
And am complete this minute

Please cedar tent of boughs embrace
My pale and chilly form
I finger needles, a pokey lace
I am at once reborn

Abigail believes in the power of creativity to grow
conscious evolution. Specializing in feminine-forward
leadership through online courses and in-person retreats,
she has worked with thousands of leaders throughout her
20 year career as a professional leadership coach. She has
spent the last 25 years helping clients developing mastery
of relational intelligence to create positive change. She
inspires spiritual truth to be lived out loud in all areas of
life. She is a passionate poetess and writer who returned to
live on the wild island where she grew up in Washington
State with her husband, Clive, their two tweening
daughters, Iona and Sophia, and her silky black lab, Bella.

RISE

Women of the Earth rise
up from the quiet landscape
swell of mountain, secret of valley
to know and be known
by that tree, that vine,
that flitting bird just off the hardened path
singing "Theeee! Theeee! Theee!"

Women of the Earth rise
beginning with skin
taking back the face,
name, breasts used to
please, placate, and pretzel
not by swift revenge, but with calm dedication
because it is the womens' work of the day

Women of the Earth rise
bow to nature's laws:
interdependence, regeneration, collaboration
laying down wide planks of story
fitting mine next to yours
and hers and hers, to become a living bridge
to walk across with raised eyes and sure feet

Women of the Earth rise
holding the spark of creation within
never to be extinguished
our fuel bright with blood
we bleed and bleed but do not die
we are the Holy Grail
never owned, and never dry

Women of the Earth rise
right action flows from
prayer inspired by nature
filling the whole world
with holy manuscript
drawing all hearts closer to
Thee! Thee! Thee!

GUNILLA NORRIS

MOON FLOWERS

I didn't know it then, the way none of us do,
what becomes of what we once planted.

In April, the seeds
went into black soil.

In May, the sprouts were gangly,
needing support.

By June, they were sent
outside to make it on their own.

They needed to thrive where they were put,
like us when we were little and not given choices.

In July, they climbed and climbed trying to get somewhere
with their heart-shaped leaves and long reaching tendrils,
greedy for support and wanting what they carved, like us.

Then on a dark moonlit evening, the first flower burst out
of its long tube of effort . . . a white, soulful blossom hung
in the humid air . . . hardly anyone noticed, same as for us.

Now in September, cascading over the privacy fence, the
spent blossoms fall to the ground below. That will continue,
no stopping it.

Same for us. But can't you hear a silent whooping at
midnight? Flowers, big as white porcelain dishes glow in the
dark, generous and willing to hold all they can. Like us, like us.

REMEMBER THIS

I feel end-time hanging in the distance while we sit silent in
our rockers on the porch.
The wet, wool-feel of August is heavy and layers up
with no way to escape the damp thickness.

Tall, and in full blossom on resolute stalks, the dahlias fold
over, drooping with the weight of
full blooming . . . deep purple-red petals bend down
in profusion as if they were shower heads.

Around us the angry sound of a mower grows closer and
seems to mow us down with
a half inch of brown grass. *Remember this,* you say,
and I nod, knowing you mean for me to treasure all this

when the killing frost comes over
the yellowing meadow, when the stubble still is upright, and
the hawks swoop by hunting field mice on their way South.
Remember. Remember, the only thing left is beginning.

Gunilla Norris, a psychotherapist in private practice for
forty-five years, has had the privilege of accompanying
many people on their journeys to growth and healing.
Her has taught meditation and led contemplative
workshops of many kinds. She has published eleven
children's books, two books of poetry and ten books on
spirituality.

WALKER ABEL

DESERT SHADE

To fall in
like a voice
into nothing it can speak—

so cool
the hot sentence of the self
stutters into silence—

and the stranded word
finds itself unwritten
in the stillness before syllables.

LIFTING ANCHOR

Once known and unknown blended like water in a stream
and I was left on the bank of a world
where ferns waver between frond and wing.

Sing a song to the moon, and it boomerangs back
with a sweetness of shadow. To the sun
and the light of years falls like a single veined leaf.

Calling and calling, the body of love
is alive with animals and rivers
with distances that burst when horizons touch.

Forever you want me to say but never is just as true
like lifting anchor from a sea that drifts
in a darkness before first phosphorescence of you.

Walker Abel, along with his partner Willow, lives at a remote off-grid home in northern California. As an undergraduate at University of California, Santa Cruz, Walker participated in an environmental studies field program called Sierra Institute. Twelve years later (1988), after completing a graduate degree with ecopsychology pioneer Robert Greenway, Walker came back to UCSC to teach for Sierra Institute, which he did for 28 years, while also taking on the role of director in 2003. Walker's first book, *The Uncallused Hand,* won the 2014 Poetry Prize from Homebound Publications. That book also went on to be a Finalist in *Foreword Reviews* 2014 Book of the Year and to win Gold in the 2015 Nautilus Awards.

APRIL TIERNEY

—

LIVING BELOW THE SURFACE

I once looked up the meaning
of depression in the dictionary.

There are several that prove unpromising
for the present state of our afflicted species

but there is one that grants me relief.

There is one that puts a hand on my flattened back
right behind my heart, and supports my weight
as I fall backwards into the blackness we've
spent a succession of lifetimes refusing to feel
in the pursuit of pure and unadulterated

unconsciousness. The definition says,
a hollowed out place in the Earth
below the surface of things.

So I hiked up a mountain and found a depression,
of which I allowed my tired body to lay down inside.
She was neither ruthless nor bottomless, actually
quite the opposite. Her basin was moist and inviting,
while her arms were round and providing.
She was nuzzled near the feet of an old pine tree
that had been turned on his side, roots reaching out
into the grasping air like tentacles or tangled cords
that had lost their use for time.

As I lay in that hole listening to people walking by
talking of pleasantries and their obsession with commonality,
I could feel the Earth breathing. I sensed her cool skin
rising and falling as she made space for my body to sink deeper
into the womb where each of our stories began. I could feel
that by resisting the downward pull, all of those other
definitions had every right to be dreadful and accurate.

But if I gave myself to it,
if I let it pull me closer
to the heart of the Earth
I might just break through

into something not yet nameable—
a spaciousness that is free of the confines
we've been instructed to behold
in order to live a life that is safe
and forever above the surface
of what is wild and true.

April Tierney is a poet, collaborative artist, activist, and lover of the world. She is the author of two full length collections of poetry, *Singing to the Bones and Origin Stories*, as well as a chapbook in collaboration with the abstract contemporary painter Will Day, entitled *The Wonder Series,* and *Exposure: Stories in Honor of Our Humanity*, a photographic anthology with Kelly Shroads. Her work has been featured in *Orion Magazine, Wild Fibers*, and *Real Ground Journal*. April lives on a deer and ponderosa pine studded hillside in Lyons, Colorado with her beautiful family.

HEIDI BARR

CONVERSATIONS

Practice being
still enough
for conversations
with wildflowers.

FORGETFULNESS

Sometimes sky and water
forget who's who
and the world remembers
what it's like to be one body.

WILDNESS

There isn't enough time
between what I've just done
and what is coming next, but
I pull into the gravel lot anyway.

I park the car and walk through a corridor
of towering pines. The wind is murmuring
as I pick my way down a rocky ravine
and slip off a sun warmed rock into cold rushing water.

Wildness swallows
the too-full day
and leaves the here and now
in its place.

Award winning author of several books, Heidi Barr is committed to cultivating ways of being that are life-giving and sustainable for people, communities and the planet. She works as a wellness coach, holds a Master's degree in Faith and Health Ministries and occasionally partners with organic farms and yoga teachers to offer retreat experiences. At home in Minnesota, she lives with her husband and daughter where they tend a large vegetable garden, explore nature and do their best to live simply.

L.M. BROWNING

IN SANTA FE WITH TIM LEARY
—for Joanna

The gutted night of Technicolor dreams
   eyes shattered like glittering ice,
     stars scattered in the vast night.

A desert hare, neither here nor there,
   heralds the pendulous horizon swing,
     pulling the moon into day and sun into night.

Lost in the eclipse
   I resurface in the dawning moonlight,
     tribal echoes pulling me through bardo.

Push-on down the abandoned routes
   where the red-tails wait like signposts
     guiding me home to the high-desert mountains.

LIKE A ROMAN CANDLE

Shame be damned
own the ruin of yourself
wear the failure like a vintage coat
   —torn, tattered heart—
   a worn out classic
soul of arcane salt and grit.

Outcast, iconoclast, standfast.
Beyond the black and white *blah*
of social norms we clash and crash
in the candle-lit dusk of conscious
dreams and darkest desires

Return to the wild
dig my heels in,
bare my teeth,
and stand this new ground.

(L.M.) Leslie M. Browning is a TEDx speaker, award-winning author, and mountain homesteader. In her writing, Browning explores the confluence of the natural landscape and the interior landscape. She holds an Associates degree in Philosophy from the University of London and a Liberal Bachelor or Arts from Harvard University focusing on English, Psychology, and Digital Media. She served on the Board of the Independent Book Publisher's Association and has been a Fellow with the International League of Conservation Writers for over 10 years. In 2011, she founded Homebound Publications & Divisions, which has since gone on to become one of the leading independent publishers in the country. She lives deep in the Berkshires of Massachusetts. When not writing or publishing the work of indie authors, she is roaming the mountains . . . which are ever-calling.

MICHAEL GARRIGAN

―

TRANSUBSTANTIATION

Nez Perce Creek, Yellowstone National Park

Sandhill cranes' short squawks seethe
at storms eclipsing this dry caldera.

A spring creek of brook trout meanders
through cracked meadows blooming with hymns

dried on tall grass lips, fumarole steam
writes wind into evaporating homilies.

Scorched bison bones chant ancient land songs
of grizzlies lying in fir and alder thickets as earth erupts.

What is knelt to in this cold volcanic dust?
What prayers let this stream run with wild trout?

How long before this land boils and burns into wilderness
incantations turning rhyolite and obsidian into another life?

WHEN HE WAS A CHINOOK SALMON

He grew a ridge of mountains
        along the edges of his mouth
as he kissed freshwater for the first
        time since he was a smolt.

His gums grew dark, his hook sharp,
        his back ridged
as he worked his way home listening
        to that dark voice behind his gill plate.

His salt scars stretch, scratched above
        his lateral line horizon,
as his mouth gulps and his caudal fin
        digs gravel beds for his seed.

He lays in shallow still water waiting
        for the bear he hears lumbering
along the bank, trying to finish the song started
        here, years ago, before he arrives,

        His world mapped on his skin.

―

Michael Garrigan writes and teaches along the Susquehanna River in Pennsylvania. He loves exploring the riverlands and believes that every watershed should have a Poet Laureate. He is the author of two poetry collections, *Robbing the Pillars* and *What I Know [How to Do]*, and was the 2021 Artist in Residence for The Bob Marshall Wilderness Area. His writing has appeared in *Orion Magazine, River Teeth*, and *The Hopper Magazine*. You can read more at www.mgarrigan.com.

J.K. MCDOWELL

. . . ANY CREATIVE LIFE.

A fresh corpse hangs in the branches and I know
I am now in the right part of the jungle forest.
The question is my Friend, where is the Jaguar?

What blight and oblivion feed his intellect?
What neglect and disregard feed her revenge?
Blades crisscross—know these are not two separate questions.

The air is thin, the spaces between are even
Thinner. Do not panic, a soft breath sometimes
Stays unnoticed by the terrors. I did say sometimes.

I turn my face away in perfect timing
As the multitude of boils on my right arm
Burst in fluidic fireworks. This is a good dream.

The engravings on this ancient skull are not
Postmortem. I wonder at the fine skill and
Psychotropics, the courage of both healer and healed.

James, I just finished reading your obituary out loud.
The portraits on the wrinkled bills in my wallet wept in grief.
No currency can lengthen the thread of any creative life.

. . . JUST REMINISCENCE.

Unnerved by the crackling ice cubes as pom juice
Blends with absinthe. Mixology points to a
Very good word to remember—reminiscence.

The converging of phantoms does not always happen
In darkness. Conjuring or summoning,
Some prefer the night light of reminiscence.

I am resigned to a poor existence as a
Prisoner of The Future. The golden chains of
Freedom can always be found in reminiscence.

Perhaps this is the physics of poetry,
We need to see future and past mingle in the
Present moment. This involves a bit of reminiscence.

Maybe he never even existed and now
I am not even here. Any ancient spell-craft
Is lost and their curses float in reminiscence.

Homebound Wayfarers might cherish the phrase:
"The Mystery Still Drives Us." *Hiraeth* is grief
And love James, and never just reminiscence.

J. K. McDowell is a poet, artist and mystic originally from the Midwest and now living in the Gulf South. Working primarily in the ghazal poetic form, his work is influenced by the American poet Robert Bly and the translations of Rumi, Hafiz, Federico Garcia Lorca and Cesar Vallejo.

AMY NAWROCKI

DISREMEMBERING

She sweeps green with a feverish broom
into the grand bassinette
of a late summer day,
then wires the sky
with golden yellow of winter wheat.

But she does not forget
the quicklime fires of twilight
and hears their weeping
in the pinhole whispers of blue.

Before the upending, the edges mattered—
the only way to hijack a hidden horizon
so the weeping could be contained.

UNLOCKED

No longer sure
that words will come
the poet thinks of motion

and commerce-filled canals
whose water rises and falls
mechanically.

She thinks of
hand-turned locks
and the crew of workers

who opened the floodgates
for barges and brass—
heaviness buoyant

as unanswered questions
and repurposed wreckage.
Down the line, water

crashes over concrete
then slows to a steady crawl.
Reed-lined banks

guard gosling nurseries
and wood ducks waddle
industriously on

rust-colored feet, rummage
in plentiful swaying grasses.
No longer doubtful

the poet finds the end,
breaks the line at
possibility.

AMY NAWROCKI

COMMONPLACE

When I am disorientated
and longing
for the company of resolve

I find myself living among fronds
next to the rock named for emptiness

every day imagining geraniums
the orientating newness
of honeysuckle.

MORTGAGE

Like the *om* of monks,
the word we have
for dwelling
vibrates through us
as we settle into it:
a wood frame
with bricks reaching
from its center, wrought
nails, glass windows,
a roof holding
us in. We've
learned by now
we do not own
this configuration
of stillness, where
cats stretch on torn-up
rugs and hands reach
toward the touchable
pages of books,
then settle
on the softness
of a cheek or fury head.
There are no loans
outstanding,
when it comes
to love, just the promise
of kisses
upon coming home.

Amy Nawrocki is the author of six collections of poetry, most recently *Mouthbrooders,* which was a finalist for the 2020 Connecticut Book Award. Her memoir *The Comet's Tail: A Memoir of No Memory* has been awarded a Gold Medal for the Living Now Mind-Body-Spirit Awards. She lives in Hamden, Connecticut with her husband and their cat, Django.

www.ingramcontent.com/pod-product-compliance
Lightning Source LLC
Chambersburg PA
CBHW052117020426
42335CB00021B/2802